THE WAR IN THE SOUTH

THE WAR IN THE SOUTH

The Carolinas and Georgia in the American Revolution

An informal history

by Donald Barr Chidsey

Illustrated

WILDSIDE PRESS

© 1969, by Donald Barr Chidsey

All pictures courtesy New York Public Library

BY THE SAME AUTHOR

HISTORY

GOODBYE TO GUNPOWDER
THE BIRTH OF THE CONSTITUTION
JULY 4, 1776
VALLEY FORGE
THE BATTLE OF NEW ORLEANS
VICTORY AT YORKTOWN
THE GREAT SEPARATION
THE TIDE TURNS
THE SIEGE OF BOSTON
THE WAR IN THE NORTH
THE GREAT CONSPIRACY
THE WAR WITH MEXICO
THE CALIFORNIA GOLD RUSH
THE FRENCH AND INDIAN WAR

BIOGRAPHY

ELIZABETH I
  A Great Life in Brief
JOHN THE GREAT
  The Times and Life of John L. Sullivan
THE GENTLEMAN FROM NEW YORK
  A Biography of Roscoe Conkling
SIR HUMPHREY GILBERT
  Elizabeth's Racketeer
SIR WALTER RALEIGH
  That Damned Upstart
MARLBOROUGH
  The Portrait of a Conqueror
BONNIE PRINCE CHARLIE
  A Biography of the Young Pretender

Contents

1 THE KIND OF WAR IT WAS   9
2 THE LAY OF THE LAND   13
3 SCOTS, WHA HAE . . .   20
4 THE RUDE BRIDGE THAT ARCHED THE FLOOD . . .   28
5 THE SOFT WALLS OF SULLIVAN   35
6 PISTOLS IN THE MORNING   49
7 THE WEAKEST LINK   56
8 IF AT FIRST YOU DON'T SUCCEED . . .   70
9 THE ALL-AMERICAN MURDERS   78
10 AN ARMY OF SCARECROWS   90
11 TOWARD THE CHESAPEAKE SQUEEZE   100
12 THE SWORD OF THE LORD AND OF GIDEON   106
13 THE STUDIOUS BLACKSMITH   116
14 HE TURNED WITH A SNARL   127
15 WHAT IS A VICTORY?   135
16 THE BIG WIPE-UP   144

   NOTES   150
   GLOSSARY OF EIGHTEENTH-CENTURY
      MILITARY TERMS   159
   BIBLIOGRAPHY   163
   INDEX   173

CHAPTER

1

The Kind of War It Was

IT HAD BEEN A BRISK LITTLE BATTLE, lasting maybe an hour; and despite the disparity in numbers—some seven hundred of the Tories, or, as they preferred to call themselves, the Loyalists, and not much more than half that many Patriots—it had been touch-and-go for a while.

This was February 14, 1779—a chilly morning.

The men were all Americans, on both sides, and most of them were from the backcountry of the Carolinas, though there were a few Georgians. The fight took place on the edge of a little stream called Kettle Creek, not far from the western bank of the Savannah, the river that separates South Carolina from Georgia.

The men, though they fought savagely, did not *look* like soldiers. They were anything but trim. The officers did not carry swords and did not mount epaulettes. Most of the men wore either buckskin or linsey-woolsey. They called themselves "militia." They carried rifles and rode plow horses, but they fought on foot, not in saddle.

The Loyalists were led by a man named Boyd, a North Carolinian, who could be cool in battle, as he was to prove, but who had not taken the simplest military precautions against surprise and who did not, it would seem, even know that there was a determined little Patriot force following him, intent upon keeping him and his men away from a junction at Augusta with Lieutenant Colonel Donald Campbell, another North Stater. On that morning of the 14th, when the Patriots came bursting out of a convenient swamp —there was always a swamp near at hand in that country— the Loyalists were in the worst possible condition.

Their arms were stacked, their horses were out at pasture, and most of the men themselves were engaged in slaughtering cattle they had taken from a plantation. It is certain that they had not paid for those cattle, and it is unlikely that they had said "please" or, afterward, "thank you." They were a predatory lot, and had left a stream of curses behind them; but there was nothing new about this, for when had soldiers ever respected private property, especially when it took the form of food?

Hit on three sides at once, the Loyalists started to scatter. Boyd pulled them together, deployed them, directed them as best he could, though the fine frenzy of that first assault was almost sure to carry the day. When Boyd himself slumped to the ground, a dying man, his followers fled. Some of them, seventy-odd, were rounded up and captured. More than forty had been killed or badly wounded. The rest either made their way to Augusta to join the war proper or, more often, by various routes went home.

The prisoners, to get them out of Campbell's reach, were taken across the Savannah into South Carolina, and there they were lined up for trial on charges of high treason. There were no lawyers present; there was no jury; and there were no summations. It was the first "war crimes" tribunal in American history, and it was conducted solemnly, if

ANDREW PICKENS

scarcely in a conventional manner—the leader of the Patriots, Andrew Pickens, being a laconic, stern Presbyterian elder.

All were found guilty; but most—for there was no place to jail them—were pardoned and set loose. Only five were condemned to die. The five were strung up then and there, for there was no provision for an appeal. They were hanged high, and they were left hanging, five corpses for the buzzards, when the Patriots broke camp next morning.

That was the way the war was, in Georgia and the Carolinas.

Wars are always dirty, especially civil wars, and this one, there, was the dirtiest yet. It pitted neighbor against neighbor, brother against brother, father against son. It was bitter right to the end, and unmarked by any touch of mercy. If there were fewer barn burnings than there had been in

New England and the middle states, where the independence forces prevailed early, this could have been only because there were fewer barns. There were more rape, more pillage, more downright murder. The threat of tarring and feathering, and sometimes the deed itself, was always present.

Perhaps because of the feathers, a frivolous appurtenance, not an integral part of the brutality, there has been for the average American something *comic* about a tar-and-feathers party. There was nothing comic about it to the victim. He was stripped naked while the tar was heated to boiling point right before his eyes. When the black, viscid stuff was slapped upon, or poured over, his body, which meant excruciating pain, nothing was spared—not even the genitals, often not even the face: men had been known to lose the sight of one or both eyes as a result of a tarring party. The man was then mounted, screaming, on a rail. He was toted out of town and dumped into a ditch, where he would lie until his friends, if he had any, ventured out to help him. It would take weeks to get the stuff entirely off and to recover fully. Emotionally, he would *never* recover.

No, tarring and feathering was not funny.

Perhaps a better epitome of the American Revolution in the Deep South, however, better than the pitiful figure of the man in the ditch, was that row of dangling bodies not far from where the fight had been at Kettle Creek.

CHAPTER

2

The Lay of the Land

THE LAY OF THE LAND is important. Actually, there was no "South" at the time of the Revolution. There were pickaninnies but no cotton picking, because there was no cotton. There might have been magnolias, but not many. White, wooden, colonnaded, porticoed plantation houses did not exist; and nobody had even heard of the mint julep.

Anything south of New York was roughly known as the South, but only so as to distinguish it from the East, which was New England. New York was simply—New York. "Middle states" was scarcely ever used.

Along the coast of the Deep South was a flat, fertile strip of land anywhere from 60 to 150 miles deep. In the northern part of the Carolinas it produced chiefly naval stores—that is, tar, pitch, turpentine, timber. In South Carolina the crops were indigo and rice. Georgia also had rice and indigo, and was beginning to experiment with silkworms; but Georgia was a thinly populated colony.

Inland of this productive strip stretched a gently rising sandy land, the red-clay country, the Pine Barrens, loblolly pine in North Carolina and the northern part of South Carolina, chiefly palmetto in southern South Carolina and in

Georgia. This led gradually to the Piedmont and in time to the mountains themselves, the Great Smokies.

The land was slashed with rivers, running northwest to southeast, mere brooks back in the hills, raging torrents near the sea, and the width and depth of these depended largely upon the weather, the rainfall. Many have picturesque names—the Pee Dee, Fishing Creek, Thicketty Creek, the Yadkin—and these vary from place to place: Troublesome Creek and Reedy Fork combine to form the Haw River; the Catawba, rising in the mountains of North Carolina, becomes the Wateree, then the Santee, under which name it falls into the sea. This can be confusing.

These streams more often than not were edged with swamps. The swamps, which might not show on a military map, could play hob with the scheduled shipment of supplies, and they were perfect lurking places for guerrillas. It was not a good land in which to fight a war.

There was no love lost between the planters of the low country on one side and the Piedmont and mountain people on the other. The one was rich; the others, poor. The plantation folks thought of themselves as cultured, perhaps even aristocratic; but the Piedmont and the mountain people had no such pretensions; quite the contrary, they were stringently homespun. Along the coast the Church of England, though not embraced with any notable fervor, was favored. The backcountry people in matters ecclesiastic were a conglomerate lot—Presbyterians, Moravians, Baptists, Dunkards, even a few Quakers—and they came originally from Germany, Scotland, Ireland, Wales. The backcountry settlers had the Indians to worry about, between 50,000 and 60,000 of them—Catawba, Cherokee, Creek, Choctaw, Chickasaw—well back in the wilderness but increasingly resentful of the way they were being pushed around. The planters did not fear the Indians, who were too far away, but they did live in daily dread of a servile uprising. There were something close to 2,000,000 slaves in the whole country below the Mason-Dixon Line, but while Negroes made up only 30 percent of the population of Maryland they were 40 percent of the population of North Carolina, 50 percent of that of South Carolina. Moreover, most of these were on plantations close to the sea. In and around Charleston the Negroes predominated by as much as six or seven to one. There were virtually no slaves in the backcountry.

When the Revolution began, there were only five cities of 8,000 or more population, and Charleston [1] was the fourth of these, after Philadelphia, New York, and Boston. It was the only city south of the Mason-Dixon Line. Virginia was the most populous colony, Massachusetts (which included Maine) the second, Pennsylvania third, and, unexpectedly, North Carolina fourth, ahead of New York.[2]

In Charleston it used to be said that there the Ashley and Cooper rivers joined to form the Atlantic Ocean. It was a highly self-conscious city, and by no means modest. Admittedly the climate was nothing to boast about: Charleston was "in the spring a paradise, in the summer a hell, in the autumn a hospital." The rich residents would go north for the summer. The slaves? Who cared?

The planters, the low-country nabobs, controlled each provincial legislature, and they meant to keep that control. Because they blocked every move on the part of the backcountry people to get a fair share of the vote, the backcountry people began to mutter in a menacing manner about taxation without representation.[3] And soon they did more than just mutter. They took the law into their own hands, organizing the first vigilante movement in America—though that word had not yet been concocted from the Spanish. They called themselves the Regulators.

There were two separate movements, two amorphous masses, though each dubbed itself the Regulators.[4]

The South Carolina Regulators spluttered that they

reached for their own law because the law would not reach to them, where they lived. The ruling politicians, they complained, made Charleston, at the southeastern tip of the state, the center of everything. They, the backcountry people, they said, had to go all the way to the capital, an arduous and expensive trip, if they wanted to find a judge, if they wanted to bring a suit or file a claim or get an official opinion or examine any records. The politicos of the coast, they charged, had so centered all the machinery of the law and of the state in Charleston that nobody would be surprised if in a little while they didn't make it a rule that anybody who wanted to answer a certain call of nature would have to go to Charleston to do so.

The wail of the North Carolina Regulators was almost the opposite. They were plagued with state officials and county officials appointed by the controlling chiefs along the seaboard. They had *too much* legal machinery, all of it imposed from the outside. These shrievalties, these assessorships and collectorships, went to men sent out by the planters, functionaries who were paid no salary but had to make their living by means of the various fees the law called for, which were many. The functionaries enforced the law to its narrowest point, collecting with both hands, for they were eager to make their pile, to get away from this sea of the great unwashed, and back to civilization. The backcountry men did not like that.

The Carolina backcountry was of course the frontier of its time, and the frontier, while it attracts many sturdy, rugged, independent-minded men, attracts also, and harbors, many a misfit, thief, fugitive from justice. In theory the Regulator movements were admirable in that they were in accord with what already was being recognized as the American spirit; but in practice they were sometimes malodorous. Not all their violence was justified, and perhaps none of it was. Personal spite played a large part in many of the activities of the Regulators.

They did not often kill a man. Usually the threat of a hot-tar party was sufficient, or an offender might be ridden out of town on a rail. The Regulators' favorite chastisement was flogging. Because there was no proper cat-o'-nine-tails to be found in those hills, recourse ordinarily was had to a length of rope, knotted and often tarred as well, so that it would bite the more viciously into bare skin. Sometimes a camp-meeting spirit prevailed at these floggings, and fiddlers played loudly while men and women danced, orgiastically excited by the screams of the victims. Sometimes, too, there was a *mass* flogging, with a whole row of victims, their bloodied backs agleam in the moonlight.

The South Carolina Regulators, though they never did make their full point, won a few of their demands, and subsided quietly. Charleston and its immediate vicinity still ran the whole state. The planters still controlled the provincial legislature.

The North Carolina Regulators went down harder, with a bang. Governor William Tryon was an ambitious man, an energetic man, and not one to temporize. He raised the North Carolina militia, and marched forth to meet the rag, tag, and bobtail Regulator forces on the banks of the Alamance. He whipped them easily—they had no artillery—and hanged six of their ringleaders. Six thousand four hundred laid down their arms, such as those were, and took an oath never to rise against the proper provincial authorities again. That ended the movement in *that* colony, though plenty of hard feeling remained.

It was 1771, just a few years before the approach of the Revolution became apparent.

It might be supposed that the rich property owners along the coast, with their traditions of culture and ease, would spurn the new talk of independence and remain staunch in support of King and Home, while the tatterdemalion, illiterate, rough-and-ready backwoodsmen would scorn the pretentious society of the seashore and come out foursquare for a new country, a new deal all around. The very opposite, at least at first, seemed to be the case, a fact that has puzzled historians.

The likeliest explanation, the one most frequently given, is that the coast men, who naturally got themselves on record before the backwoodsmen, on the whole plumped for the new cause, not because of any exalted ideas about freedom but because of sound reasons of trade; and that the backcountry men, seeing this, went the *other* way out of sheer spite. This is open to question.[5]

In a widely quoted passage [6] John Adams, who had as much to do with bringing about the Revolution as any man and who certainly was an astute observer, wrote that at the opening of hostilities about one-third of the population of the colonies was in favor of independence, one-third was opposed, and the rest didn't care one way or the other. This was a judgment reached many years after the event, but it is probably correct.[7]

Passions were hot, and there was a great deal of namecalling, while the poor neutral, who asked only to be left alone, was execrated by right and left alike.

The Patriots called themselves that, proudly; but the Loyalists called them rebels. The Loyalists were known among the Patriots as Tories, the Patriots among the Tories as Whigs, but in fact there was never any organization comparable in the smallest way with the new two-party system in Great Britain. There were other names, on each side, and they were not pretty.

In the nature of the problem there could be no statistics, only opinions; but it was agreed that the most loudly Loyalistic of the colonies were New York and North Caro-

The Lay of the Land 19

lina. Neither was as heavily weighted to the Loyalist cause as its governor would have had the men in Whitehall believe, and a fifty-fifty division in each case would not be too far amiss.[8] In any event, the Revolution in its early days was by no means the overwhelmingly popular uprising that many generations of American schoolchildren have been taught to believe.[9]

The British seized New York early, in an assault that greatly hurt and all but wiped out the Continental Army, and they were to hold it—the city, that is, the port—for the rest of the war. They foraged extensively the length of Long Island, and they raided, again and again, Westchester County and even as far north as Dutchess County; but for all intents and purposes, and except spottily, for all the fact that in Canada they controlled the entire northern border of the colony, they could not occupy and hold any part of upstate. Their power extended just exactly as far as their muskets could carry.

North Carolina was a different matter. It had no city, no seaport worth mentioning. It had no thickly settled district, no point of control. The distances were great, the swamps dismal, the frontier wild. Nevertheless, the British were to try to grab and govern North Carolina. They were to try very hard.

CHAPTER

3

Scots, Wha Hae . . .

MEN IN AMERICA were Loyalists for many reasons, none of them regional.

There were the officeholders, whose very livelihood depended upon the predominance of the crown, and their friends, those who liked the feeling of "official" society, and of course their dependents. These were largely confined to the cities, the ports.

There were the Anglican clergymen, who represented an established church and who in the North and in the middle states almost to a man were pro-king, anti-independence. In the South this was not so.

There were the naturally conservative, who had as much as they could hope to get and were determined to hold on to it. However, it is to be remarked that not all the wealthy men clung to the Parliamentary party. John Hancock, Charles Carroll of Carrollton, and George Washington might have been the three richest men in America, and each was a dedicated advocate of independence.

There were the irritated Tories, who were Tories for no other reason than that they resented the Patriots' effort to dominate the political scene, Tories who, that is, refused to be pushed around.

There were the dynastic Tories, the legality Tories, the religious Tories.

And finally, as Van Tyne notes, "there were the factional Tories, whose action was determined by family feuds and old political animosities." [10]

Residents of occupied territory for the most part decided, in the phrase of the time, to be "on the side of the hangman"; but this was not so in the Deep South, where everybody knew his neighbor's opinions. The section, if it had its outspoken Loyalists, had outspoken Whigs as well. It was in the quaint little village of Charlotte, North Carolina—two streets, thirty residences, a courthouse—that Mecklenburg County representatives as early as May 31, 1775, immediately after the arrival of the news of Lexington and Concord, adopted a declaration of independence, the first, the so-called Mecklenburg Declaration, more than a year before the famous one adopted by the Continental Congress in Philadelphia.[11]

North Carolina was also the first state to authorize its delegates to the Second Continental Congress to vote for independence. South Carolina was a close second.[12]

Georgia was the only colony not represented at the First Continental Congress, but this was largely because the sparsely populated place at that time was threatened by an uprising of the Creeks to the west, and could not spare the manpower. To the *Second* Continental Congress Georgia sent a small but strong delegation, consisting of George Walton, Lyman Hall, and Button Gwinnett, all of whom signed the Declaration of Independence.

The framing of that Declaration was made possible by the submission to Congress of three resolutions, on June 7, 1776, by Richard Henry Lee:

"That these United Colonies are, and of a right ought

to be, free and independent States, that they are absolved from all allegiance to the British Crown, and that all political connection between them and the State of Great Britain is, and ought to be, totally dissolved.

"That it is expedient forthwith to take the most effectual measures for forming foreign Alliances.

"That a plan of confederation be prepared and transmitted to the respective Colonies for their consideration and approbation."

Lee was a Virginian, but it was the North Carolina delegation that moved the acceptance and consideration of these resolutions, and the South Carolina delegation seconded the motion.

Southerners had no personal fondness for the residents of New England, whom they found coarse and arrogant, men who talked through their noses and believed that theirs was a monopoly on piety; while the "Wise Men of the East" for their part regarded Southerners as pompous, full of their own importance. Yet when Parliament passed the Boston Port bill to punish that city for the Tea Party of December 16, 1773, Boston did not hesitate to call upon the southern colonies for help, nor did the southern colonies fail to respond. Within a few weeks of the time the news had been received, more than two hundred barrels of rice were on their way to Massachusetts from the ports of Savannah and Charleston; and this was only the beginning.

Opposition to the Stamp Act and to the tax on tea was every bit as strong in the Deep South as in New England, if it was not as noisy.[13]

In the summer of 1775, just after the outbreak of hostilities in Massachusetts, the colonies of Virginia and Maryland sent four companies of backcountry riflemen to the Continental camp at Cambridge, and these men took a prominent part in the arduous Montgomery-Arnold invasion of Canada.

There were several reasons why the Carolinas and Georgia did not follow suit. The distance, for one thing, was greater. The backcountry situation in the Deep South was much different, and it was by no means certain at first how many Loyalists there might be who were willing to take up arms. Finally, and most important, Georgians and Carolinians had good reasons to believe that their own land was about to be invaded.

William Tryon had been transferred to the royal governorship of New York, a much more lucrative job, and he was succeeded by another energetic, not to say pugnacious, person, Josiah Martin. Martin was florid and emphatic. Alarmed by all the stirrings of the Patriots about him, he sent his pregnant wife and their several children off to New York, and on the same ship he sent a request to General Gage, the British commander in chief in America, for 10,000 stands of arms, six brass 6-pounders, and a colonel's commission.

Martin's scheme was grandiose. He planned not only to keep his own colony steady but to take over the whole of the Deep South, and perhaps the Chesapeake region as well, and hold these in the name of the king. This he proposed to do by means of the muskets and fieldpieces to be shipped from Boston and with the help of two large bodies of Loyalists in inland North Carolina.

The first of these bodies was what remained of the Regulators. *Martin* had not hanged their leaders, and was, he believed, he hoped, on good terms with them. The other body was the flourishing Cross Creek settlement of Highland Scots. Martin might have had some doubts about the loyalty of the Regulators, but he really believed that the Highlanders would stay faithful to the last man. He said this, repeatedly.

The Highlanders need some explanation. For more than forty years they had been pouring into America, and principally into North Carolina. It was a craze in the Highlands, and like most crazes it was of unknown origin. Thoughts of the New World haunted the imaginations of the Highlanders, who could talk of little else. In one island, Skye, they even had a dance called the America.

There are those who blithely aver that it was the stamping out of the Young Pretender's uprising of 1745–1746 that resulted in this immigration from the lochs and glens of northern Scotland to the dunes of North Carolina, but the movement demonstrably had been started more than twenty years before that uprising, and there is no evidence that any Highlander ever was exiled because of his pro-Stuart stand.

The years immediately after the Bonnie Prince Charlie uprising were not notable for Scottish transatlantic voyages —quite the contrary. It was not until just before the beginnings of the American Revolution, and especially the years 1773 and 1774, that the great influx of Highland Scots was recorded. It might be worth mentioning, too, that an overwhelming majority of the Highlanders who made the trip to North Carolina came either from the Western Isles or from Inverness, neither of which had contributed notably to the support of Charles Edward Stuart, *or* from Argyll, the biggest contributor. Now, Argyll is Campbell country, and the Campbells as a clan had not only failed to respond to Prince Charles's call but had actually taken the field against him.

Though the Highlanders were not being punished, their economy was being twisted every which way, and it could be that the drastic measures adopted by the British government after the 1745 uprising had something to do with bringing about the conditions that made clansmen look with longing upon America. Military roads had been built into and through the previously almost inaccessible Highlands. These roads were designed to make another such insurrection impossible or at least highly inadvisable, but one of their principal results was the opening up to the Lowland sheepherders property that had hitherto been the domain of the Highland cattlemen, who were thus crowded out. Also, there was the breaking up of the clan system, another action taken because of the Prince Charles uprising. Suddenly, and for the first time in their history, clansmen were free of feudal obligations, and could go wherever they wished without first getting the permission of their chiefs. Anybody who had the ship fare of £3 10s—half of that for a child under eight—could emigrate to America, being tolerably sure of getting a large grant of public lands once he got there.

It was this gubernatorial power to dispense with public lands that had given Martin his hold over a large number of the displaced Highlanders, all those who had flocked to North Carolina just after the transfer of Tryon. He had warned them, *en masse*, that he would not hand out any real estate until the immigrants had first taken an oath of allegiance to the House of Hanover, adding that any who broke this oath would have his land expropriated. Thousands had taken the oath, perforce, having no money with which to get back. There was, for instance, Allan Macdonald, a middle-aged man of quiet dignity, who had with him his wife, Flora Macdonald, the heroine of the Bonnie Prince Charlie escape legend. Macdonald had been granted five hundred good acres in the Cape Fear district. He would not be likely to jeopardize them.

There were also Stewarts, Campbells, MacLeods, McLeans, MacArthurs, and others.[14]

These men, known to be stout warriors, did not go unwooed. The Second Continental Congress had sent emissaries among them in order to ascertain their political views. These emissaries had failed to get far, because so few of the Scots spoke English, while Gaelic was not a tongue to be picked up overnight.

General Gage sent two real Scots, men who *could* speak

ROBERT HOWE

Gaelic, similarly to sound out the Cross Creek colonists. These were Donald Macdonald and Donald McLeod, officers, both of whom had been slightly wounded in the battle for Bunker Hill. The Committee of Safety of New Bern, alarmed, soon after these men arrived in North Carolina had called them up for questioning. What was their purpose in being here? McLeod and Macdonald blandly explained that they were no longer connected with the British Army and they had come to the Cross Creek country [15] only in order to visit with some relatives and friends. They were released.

Meanwhile, Governor Martin had decided that things were not safe at the Executive Mansion, and he retired to Fort Johnson on the Cape Fear River. It was not much of a haven. The garrison of twenty-odd had recently been cut in half by desertions, and there was scarcely any gunpowder left. When the Wilmington Committee of Safety formally announced that it meant to raze the fort, Martin and the remains of the garrison retreated to the sloop-of-war *Cruizer*, from the deck of which, on July 18, they watched the fort burned by one of its former commanders, Colonel Robert Howe, a wealthy and well-educated young planter who was also an ardent Patriot.[16]

Martin, subsisting on salted rations aboard the *Cruizer*, was uncomfortable but not abashed. On January 3, 1776, he got his authorization (though not the colonelcy he had asked for) from London. He immediately summoned Anson, Cumberland, Chatham, Guilford, Mecklenburg, Rowan, Surry, and Bute counties, to rally around the royal standard. The new troops should then make for the coast, where they would be met by powder- and musket-carrying ships from British headquarters in Boston and by troop transports from Ireland. They should get to the coast not later than February 15.

It was about this time that Martin was reported to have issued a call for a slave insurrection, promising to arm the Negroes. He denied this, but it was commonly believed, and it hurt his cause. His neighbor to the north, Governor John Murray, Lord Dunmore, had issued such a call, and with it had ruined any chance he might have had to hold down the Patriot cause in his colony. Dunmore, too, had taken refuge aboard an offshore warship, as indeed had done the royal governors of South Carolina and Georgia. Not one of these four men dared to put his foot on the ground.

Nevertheless Josiah Martin leaned back, satisfied. He was confident that the Highlanders of Cross Creek would rise.

He was right. They did.

CHAPTER

4

The Rude Bridge That Arched the Flood . . .

THE BRIDGE OVER Moore's Creek was about eighteen miles north of Wilmington, a port strongly held by the Patriots but threatened from the outside, from the sea, by the omnipotent Royal Navy. It was an uninspiring structure made of pine, and it was situated on a sandbar, the highest point of land in the middle of a swamp. The creek itself, which empties into the Black River about ten miles above its confluence with the Cape Fear River, was about fifty feet wide at that point, and it was only about five feet deep, except in times of much rain; but it was fast-moving, and the bottom was treacherous with black mud. It belonged to a man named James Hepburn, but it was not a toll bridge and there was no habitation near it. The only regular residents of that neighborhood were the cottonmouth moccasins.

Governor Martin, in his proclamation of January 10, 1776, had called upon the Loyalists to put down "the most horrid and unnatural rebellion that has been exerted in the Province . . . by traitorous, wicked and designing men," but the enthusiasm was his alone. The Highlanders, though

The Rude Bridge That Arched the Flood ... 29

they answered the summons promptly, carrying what weapons they had, mostly heavy Scottish claymores and the deadly *skene dhu*, a dirk half hidden in a stocking, and though they wore the kilt and thrilled to the squeal of the pipes, were by no means sure what this was all about. Virtually all of them were "newly-outs," men who had signed Martin's pledge, and they believed that they were only protecting their property when they answered the call. There were no harangues, no huzzas, not much music, and no dancing at all. The Highlanders, trained for centuries in obedience, bowed to the old adage of "A new lord, new laws," but plainly they did not like the smell of the business.

They camped about four miles south of Cross Creek, and elected Allan Macdonald, Flora's husband, their military chief for the moment. This was more or less an honorary post, a decorative post. Macdonald had fought at Culloden, but he was not a trained soldier. He was middle-aged, and in poor health. The real heads of the little army were the two veterans of Bunker Hill, Donald Macdonald and Donald McLeod, as colonel and his adjutant respectively.

The quondam Regulators were more outspoken with their own reluctance. Only a few came, not nearly as many as Martin had expected—he had boasted that he could raise 2,000 ex-Regulators alone—and from the beginning they showed a tendency to slip away, something they found it easy to do, for they knew the country well.

There was bad feeling between the two groups. The Regulators, greatly in the minority, resented having to assemble in Highlander territory. These Johnny-come-latelies couldn't even speak English! The Regulators were bewildered, and not at all amused by the glitter and the gabble, by the sporrans, the tartans, and those earsplitting bagpipes. The Highlanders, they soon learned, were a melancholy lot, forever lamenting their exile in a foreign land, forever chanting lugubrious dirges—those few that you could understand at all:

> "O where shall I gae seek my bread?
> Or where shall I gae wander?
> O where shall I gae hide my head?
> For here Ill bide nae langer.
> The seas may row, the winds may blow,
> And swathe me round in danger;
> My native land I must forego
> And roam a lonely stranger." [17]

Anybody who would spout stuff like that was not the kind of man you'd want by your side in a fight, now was he?

Their numbers were uncertain. No record was kept, and many men were to deny, later, that they had been "out." They were coming and going so rapidly that even the leaders did not know how many the whole force numbered—probably about 1,500, of whom about 1,300 were Highlanders.

Meanwhile, Colonel Howe's regiment being in nearby Virginia, where an invasion at Norfolk was feared, Colonel James Moore assembled his 1st North Carolina Continentals, about 650 men and five guns. On February 15 they marched out of Wilmington, to camp that night on the banks of Rockfish Creek, only about seven miles from the Highlander-Regulator camp. Here they were joined in the next few days by Colonel Alexander Lillington with 150 minutemen (the minuteman system was practiced in the South as well as in New England, though it was never accorded so much publicity), Colonel Kennon with 200 men, and 100 Partisan Rangers under Colonel John Ashe.

The commanding officers now waxed Cervantic.

Donald Macdonald sent Colonel Moore a copy of Governor Martin's proclamation, together with a friendly but

The Rude Bridge That Arched the Flood . . .   31

firm letter urging him to rally to the royal standard, all this, of course, under a flag of truce.

Moore, under another flag, sent Macdonald a copy of the Test Oath the local Committee of Safety had drawn up, and suggested that he and all his men subscribe to this and avoid bloodshed by joining the Patriot army.

Neither accepted the other's invitation.

Macdonald's wish was to get to the rendezvous at Brunswick, across the river from Wilmington, without having to fight. Moore's plan was to prevent it.

Colonel Richard Caswell with about 800 Partisan Rangers was approaching the scene from the direction of New Bern. He sent a message to Moore, reporting that the Scots had crossed the Black River, going straight east, and were nearing Moore's Creek. Moore sent off Lillington and Ashe to Moore's Creek, ordered Caswell there as well, and himself started a long hook that he hoped would bring him with the main body down upon the Highlanders' rear, at the same time blocking the route to Cape Fear.

Ashe and Lillington got to the bridge on the night of the 25th. Next day they started to erect breastworks and dig trenches on the east side of the bridge, but soon Caswell came along with his two fieldpieces, and took command. Caswell started to throw up breastworks on the *west* side of the bridge, the side the Scots, still hidden in the swamp, could be assumed to be approaching. However, Caswell changed his mind after a little while, and ordered the entrenchment work on the west bank to be abandoned. He retired with all his men, perhaps 1,100 of them, to the east bank, the side toward the sea, where he strengthened the defense works Ashe and Lillington had already built and where he mounted his two cannons, which were called, for no reason that survives, Old Mother Covington and Her Daughter.

As they crossed, they took up a large number of the boards near the middle of the bridge, leaving only the round stringpieces, which they smeared with soap and bear's grease.

That night, a dark one, the Highlanders came to the west bank. Caswell's men could hear them over there, whispering, clinking, arguing. It was, it would seem, a scouting party. It was not challenged.

Farther back in the swamp the Scottish officers conferred. The scouts, who must have been blind, reported that the entrenchments on the west bank had been left as they were and had not even been filled in, from which they deduced that the rebels had retreated. They had heard nothing from the other bank, and had glimpsed no fire there. They did not say that a big portion of the bridge was missing in the middle, and it could be that they had not even noticed the fact.

The officers were split. The older ones, the professionals, the Bunker Hill men, would have preferred to wait until daylight, in order to make *sure* that there were no entrenchments on the far side of the creek, but the younger men, hotheaded, were all for an immediate attack.

One of the most fervent of these young men was Alexander McLeod, who only the other day had married the daughter of Allan and Flora Macdonald, a girl whom he had literally left at the altar in order to go to war. He offered to lead the advance guard. Captain John Campbell made the same offer. They won their point after throwing out hints of cowardice in the somewhat small-boyish manner of so many green soldiers. The older officers, against their own better judgment, gave in.

An advance guard of eighty men was carefully picked. They were armed only with claymores and dirks, all they asked, the weapons their forefathers had used. Of course, they had pipers to accompany them.

The bridge was only six miles away. They reached it a

The Rude Bridge That Arched the Flood . . . 33

little before dawn. They drew their broadswords, shouted their slogans, and charged.

It was magnificent but it was not war.

The Patriots, perfectly prepared, let loose with muskets, rifles, and fieldpieces. It was all over in a few minutes. Some of the men got across, not many. Most of them either were shot down on the bridge or slipped off the stringpieces and fell into the water, or else they broke, and turned and ran, bringing panic into the main body.

The two leaders were among those who got across, but they were quickly shot. McLeod had got nearest to the Patriot entrenchments, only a few yards off. Nine balls and twenty-four pieces of swan shot [18] were plucked out of his corpse. The Macdonald girl never saw her husband again.

Though nothing was done about a pursuit that day, it is hard to see why. Not until Colonel Moore came to take command, early the next morning, was such a pursuit organized. It was phenomenally successful. The ex-Regulators for the most part got away; but the Highland Scots, strangers in a strange land, and easily lost, were gathered together in great groups, most of them glad of the chance to surrender. They were treated well. The "war crimes" phase of the Revolution in the Deep South had not yet begun; nobody was hanged.

The pursuit parties brought in thirteen wagons complete with horses, a war chest containing £15,000 in specie, 1,500 rifles, 350 muskets, 150 swords and dirks. Not all of these had been thrown away on the field or taken from prisoners. Some came out of Tories' houses in the neighborhood, which the Patriots did not hesitate to search and to strip.

The Loyalists lost something between fifty and seventy dead, wounded, and drowned. The Patriots lost two wounded, one of whom later died.

Moore's Creek Bridge has been called "the Lexington

and Concord of the South." This is a distortion; but the tussle, however one-sided, did have a tremendous effect upon the spirits of the Patriots in those parts. If the Scots had made it to the coast, the war might have had a different ending. For General Clinton, down from Boston, actually did land nine hundred regulars in Brunswick County. When he learned of the battle at the bridge, there was nothing for him to do but order the men back into their transports, and to head for Charleston, leaving North Carolina alone.[19]

CHAPTER

5

The Soft Walls of Sullivan

THE BRITISH GRAND STRATEGY, a chameleon, was of incalculable help to the American cause. At the beginning of the war its conduct was part of the duties of the secretary of state for colonies. He was an earl named Dartmouth, an amiable man from all accounts, but no genius. For reasons not apparent to the layman, it was decided toward the end of the year 1775 that there must be a cabinet shake-up. Dartmouth was shifted to the Privy Seal, while his place was taken by Lord George Germain.

Here was a curious choice. Germain had connections, though few friends. He had once been in the army and had been head of the British horse at Minden, where, when ordered, he refused to charge. For this he had been cashiered, cast out, and declared to be unfit to serve the king in any capacity whatever. Now, through the vagaries of British politics, he was authorized to conduct a war on the other side of the sea in a land he had never seen. All the high officers of the army, it should be noted, abhorred him.

Germain did not get along with Guy Carleton, governor and commander in chief of Canada. He did not get along with Major General William Howe, who had succeeded Gage as commander in chief in the other colonies. He was soon to be bitterly embroiled with Major General Henry Clinton, Howe's second-in-command.

The war dragged. It was already more than half a year old, and it cost a lot of money. Howe's troops, cooped in Boston, could do nothing. Even if they broke out of that port, they could not penetrate any telling distance into the interior because they did not have the transportation. They must be reinforced and resupplied. It was Howe's own idea that they could refit at nearby Nova Scotia and then descend upon New York, which they would seize, placing themselves astride the line of the colonies right about at the middle. Germain approved this; but he also approved the Cape Fear Plan.

He had not devised the Cape Fear Plan but had inherited it. Dartmouth while still in the colonial post had committed the government to it. In doing so, Dartmouth had been swayed by the royal governors of the various southern colonies, each of whom confidently predicted that large numbers of his constituents would rally around the flag as soon as that flag was displayed. Furthermore, winter was a good time for operations in the South, though nothing much could be done in the North during that time.

Cape Fear, North Carolina, would be the trysting place. A small army would be sent there from Boston, and would meet or be met by a fleet of transports from Ireland. The navy, hopefully, would cooperate. An immediate thrust into the interior would be made, as far at least as the Cross Creek country, where many thousands of Loyalists would offer their services as soldiers. However, if anything went wrong, the commander could still turn to the Chesapeake country—Virginia and Maryland—where he could establish a British naval base and cut the colonies in half at *that* point. Or, depending upon how he found local conditions, he could turn south, besiege and take Charleston, and from there easily overspread the whole of the Deep South.

Howe protested that this would take away a large part of his command when what he needed, and had been promised, was reinforcements. He was overruled, for it was pointed out that he remained in command and could call the Cape Fear force back any time he pleased. Miffed, he gave in. At least he could and did appoint Clinton to head the force. It would be good to get rid of Clinton for a while. Howe simply couldn't bear the man; and this was odd, because while Clinton was thin-skinned and touchy, Howe himself was easygoing, the very soul of affability.

Clinton left Boston on January 20. Washington, besieging the city, watched him go, as he had watched the preparations for this departure. Washington already had warned the Continental Congress, saying that he believed that a descent upon New York was planned, though it could be, he conceded, a descent upon Virginia. He did not seem to think that Charleston might be threatened. Washington also sent his second-in-command, Major General Charles Lee, to New York.

Lee was a scarecrow, cantankerous, acidulous, arrogant, breathlessly ugly, as jerky as a quockerwodger, but he knew more about the art of war, as it was breathlessly called, than anybody else in America—anybody, that is, on the Continental side. He had a dazzling European record, and was considered a lucky find by the Continentals.

Lee rode through Connecticut to arrive in New York City at the same time as the seagoing Clinton. Clinton's appearance brought about a panic, even after he had solemnly promised the inhabitants that he did not mean to land, only to confer with Governor Tryon, whom he invited to his flagship.

Lee, unruffled, made a survey of the possible defenses. He submitted a masterly report to Congress, for the man, for all his eccentricities, really did know his business. He suggested certain temporary measures, but he insisted that in the long run it would be impossible to defend the water-girt city from any British amphibious force. If Congress had listened to this advice, much misery would have been saved.

Lee then was about to start north, for Congress had appointed him to the command of the Northern District, to succeed Philip Schuyler, when Congress reversed itself and appointed him instead to the command of the newly created *Southern* District. So he went south.

Congress, incidentally, did all this without consulting the so-called commander in chief, George Washington.

In Virginia, in the governor's mansion at Williamsburg, Lee paused, wondering whether to stay there or to proceed farther south. An intercepted message helped him.

A privateer captain, James Barron, had caught a dispatch carrier, and by means of a letter from Lord Germain to Governor Robert Eden of Maryland the Continental authorities at last were enabled to learn about the Cape Fear Plan.

It was to be no mere casual coastal raiding party, this jaunt of Clinton's. It was to be the real thing.

Leaving Cork, Ireland, some time early in February, to head for Cape Fear and the connection with Clinton, were to be ten war vessels, under Admiral Sir Peter Parker, and more than thirty transports with about 2,500 regular troops under Lord Cornwallis.

Still, General Lee was in doubt. He lingered a little at Williamsburg, feeling "like a dog at a dancing-school," as he wrote to a friend, not knowing which way to turn. At last he ventured down to Wilmington, North Carolina.

Clinton, himself late, found no Irish fleet waiting for him at the cape. He soon learned that the original idea, of marching inland at that point, was better abandoned. He learned, that is, about the affair at Moore's Creek Bridge.

The Soft Walls of Sullivan

The Patriots were terrorizing the countryside, and Loyalists would not even dare to give three muffled cheers for King George in the privacy of their own cellars.

Sir Peter Parker's ships started only a little late, but five days out they were scattered by a storm and had to put back to Cork or, some of them, to Plymouth or Portsmouth. Refitted, they set forth again, after a while—only to run into another bad blow. It was late April before the first of them began to appear off Cape Fear, and early May before the last had reported.

Sir Peter and the general conferred. It had been the general's opinion that the rebellion could best be stamped out by squeezing the "waist" of the colonies, the Chesapeake area, but now he seems to have allowed himself to be talked into a plan to take Charleston instead, the plan Sir Peter favored.

So they went to Charleston. And General Lee hurried by land to the same place, arriving, once again, on the very same day that the ships were sighted. He was "hasty and rough in his manners, which the officers could not reconcile themselves to at first."[20] He was openly impatient with soldiers who did not know a ravelin from a saucisson, a redan from a tenaille, and who doubtless thought that a cohorn was some sort of band instrument. He started to tell everybody how everything should be done. Nevertheless, he gave a great boost to the defenders' spirit, he was so sure of himself.

The usual population of Charleston, the metropolis of the South, was 12,000. Many of these, virtually all the able-bodied males, white or Negro, were among the defenders, who numbered, it was estimated, about 6,000. More than 100 cannons were placed. Warehouses along the waterfront were razed in order to give the balls clearance and to reduce the danger of hot shot. The Patriot governor, John Rutledge, was everywhere. Charleston was a sporting city, but for the duration of the siege it was agreed that gambling and horse racing should be taboo; they were frivolities unsuited to a crisis.

The offing at this point is stippled with small flat low islands, separated from one another and from the mainland by inlets or creeks or estuaries, salt water for the most part, and shallow. Many contained swamps in their centers, and these were interlaced with other creeks. They were covered with palmettos, myrtle, and other low shrubs, and here and there a live oak.

Two such islands, rather larger than the average, guarded the narrow entrance of the channel that led to Charleston proper, some six miles from the open sea. If ever a warship got through that channel, and could put the city under its guns, all the Patriots with all the high spirits in the world wouldn't have made a difference.

To the south was James Island, protected by what had been a royal stronghold, Fort Johnson. The provincial soldiery had seized it during the previous September, when they kicked the royal governor out. The fort mounted twenty guns, 18- and 25-pounders, and on the same island not far away, nearer the city itself, was a battery of twelve heavy guns.

To the north was Sullivan's Island, about four miles long, at high tide barely one mile wide. At the southern end of this island the Patriots had begun to construct Fort Sullivan, the city's principal hope; but it was barely half finished. In such a position, defying naval guns, the fort should have been constructed of the heaviest stone, but no such stone had been available at the time, and palmetto logs had been used instead. These were set in a large square, each side consisting of two walls sixteen feet apart, lashed together at regular intervals by other palmetto logs, the center being filled with sand. There were supposed to be four palmetto bastions, one at each corner, but only the east and the south ones had been completed. To the north and to the west the fort had no protection but a series of low earthworks. If at-

The Soft Walls of Sullivan 41

WILLIAM MOULTRIE

tacked by land—that is, if landing parties could get behind it—it would fall in a matter of minutes, with no fieldpieces needed. If attacked by sea, with the big guns the British could bring to bear, it might as well be that much pasteboard. So said artillery expert after artillery expert, and especially the naval ones. Still, Governor Rutledge loved his Fort Sullivan and would not hear of its abandonment. It was commanded by William Moultrie, who had thirty guns and a little over four hundred militiamen.

General Lee, leaping about, shook his head when he saw Fort Sullivan. He "did not like that part at all," calling it a "slaughter-pen," and he expostulated to Governor Rutledge, who, however, refused to order the abandonment of the place. The governor controlled the militia, and Lee controlled only the Continental troops, so the governor won.

Lee said: "Colonel Moultrie, do you think you can maintain this post?" And Moultrie replied: "Yes, I think I can." And "that was all that passed on the subject between us."[21] But Lee was still shaking his head when he went away.

The wind was with the Patriots. Sir Peter Parker's warships and Clinton's and Cornwallis's transports had come into sight of Charleston June 4, but it was not until the 12th that they could venture close to the channel opening, and even then they could not get close enough to open an effective fire. The war vessels, with their heavy guns, their big crews, and their huge stocks of powder and shot, drew much more water than ordinary merchant vessels.

Another try was made on the 25th, but this also failed. The defenders were given just that much more time to tighten their positions and to bring up supplies.

It was not until June 28 that the big fighters *Bristol* and *Experiment*, each fifty guns, and *Active*, *Thunder*, *Friendship*, and *Solebay*, almost as large, were got over the bar, together with the frigates *Actaeon*, *Sphinx*, and *Syren*.

The British had not been idle all that while. Soundings had been taken, so that the captains learned what kind of gut they were about to traverse. General Clinton had landed 900 light infantrymen on Long Island, just to the north of Sullivan's, and soon afterward he had increased this to 2,500. His idea was to take the fort from behind, and he had been given to understand that Long Island, which was deserted, was separated from Sullivan's Island only by a narrow estuary called the Breach, and that the Breach was only eighteen inches deep, so that men could wade it. It turned out that the Breach was indeed only eighteen inches deep—in places. In other places it was seven feet deep. Clinton began losing men right and left. Heavily laden, they would simply drop out of sight. Boats were not the answer because the shallow spots were too shallow. Hence, Clinton's 2,500 were stranded

The Soft Walls of Sullivan 43

on Long Island, looking foolish, and had nothing to do with the battle.

Clinton did signal to Admiral Parker, asking if he could be of help in any other way. But the admiral did not answer, doubtless because he wished to keep the thing a naval show. Interservice rivalry was never more blatant.

It was eleven o'clock in the morning when the bombardment began. Nobody, not even the British veterans, had heard anything like it. Any naval expert could have told you, on the spot, that nothing, absolutely nothing, could stand up against such a shower of metal for more than an hour or two; and he could have backed this assertion with figures.[22]

The range was about 400 yards—for guns of that size, virtually point-blank.

The men on Sullivan's Island fought back. Indeed, just at first they fought back too hard. The supply of gunpowder there was low, and Moultrie had to devote all his energies to the task of making the gunners fire less often and more accurately. Every shot must count. They soon achieved a smooth regularity, which they kept up all that afternoon, an astounding performance. Long after they should have been buried in debris, the gunners of Fort Sullivan still were firing with beautiful regularity—and deadly aim.

They concentrated on the nearest and biggest of the battleships, *Bristol* and *Experiment*, especially *Bristol*, Parker's flag. Early in the action *Bristol*'s cable was shot away, and the tide swung her end-on to the fort, which raked her from stern to bow again and again, inflicting terrible damage. Seventy balls hulled her. The top of her mainmast was carried away. Her mizzen was so slashed by 32-pound shot that it had to be axed off. Before she could be straightened to a broadside position by means of another cable, her decks had been swept clear of all living. Had there been any kind

THE DEFENSE OF SULLIVAN'S ISLAND—JUNE 28, 1776

The Soft Walls of Sullivan   45

of sea running she would surely have sunk. As it was, she kept fighting.

The frigates *Sphinx, Syren,* and *Actaeon* now proceeded to try to sneak into the harbor under cover of this terrific bombardment. In order to get out of the range of the guns at Fort Sullivan, where the move had been observed, the frigates went too far south; and they slid up on a sandbar, fast. This was a great piece of luck for the Patriots. If those frigates had ever got into the harbor, they could have battered Fort Sullivan to pieces, hitting its unprotected sides.

All this time General Clinton and his 2,500 on Long Island were doing absolutely nothing; for there was nothing that they could do, except slap mosquitos.

Once, early in the afternoon, the light blue-and-white flag that flew from the Fort Sullivan pole went down. What did that mean? Was the garrison surrendering?

The garrison was doing no such thing. The flag had been shot down, a lucky hit. It fluttered through an embrasure and settled upon the land below, outside the wall. Sergeant William Jasper scrambled through the embrasure, retrieved it, climbed back into the fort, and shinnied up a jury pole to nail it fast—all this under heavy fire. A great cheer went up.

Wood splinters in sea battles often killed more men than cannon balls. General Lee had cried that Fort Sullivan would not last half an hour under a British naval bombardment, and if the fort had been made of oak or even of some brittle stone undoubtedly he would have been proved right. But palmetto is a soft, porous wood. It offered no resistance to the balls, but simply swallowed them, and they got lost in the sandy expanses within. Now and then a ball would shriek through one of the embrasures, and when that happened somebody was almost sure to be hit; but most of them poofed harmlessly into that great spongy mass of wood and sand. Some sailed over the walls, to plop into what would have

SERGEANT WILLIAM JASPER REPLACING THE FLAG

been the middle of the yard if there had been a real, whole fort; and these sank into a morass there, hurting no one.

After the fight some 7,000 balls were recovered in and around Fort Sullivan; but there must have been many that never were found.

Moultrie was beginnng to run out of powder, and for a little while, late in the afternoon, it looked as though he might have to spike his guns and make his way as best he could to the mainland. But Lee got 700 pounds more to him, and the guns of the fort spoke again.

Syren and *Sphinx* got off the sandbar somehow, but they were crippled. *Actaeon* was immovable, and her crew—first setting her on fire, of course—abandoned her in small boats.

The firing slacked off a bit at sunset, and at nine thirty it stopped. At eleven o'clock the British warships slipped

The Soft Walls of Sullivan   47

their cables and drifted out with the tide. No captain among them had any thought of continuing the siege. It would take them weeks of work just to patch their parts.

On the *Bristol* alone there were 64 dead and 161 wounded.

Moultrie had lost perhaps a dozen killed and about twice that many wounded.

As for General Clinton, he and his men had to be taken off Long Island piecemeal, as the opportunity offered. There was no question of *his* renewing the siege either, even if the navy had been prepared to help. He was under strict orders from General Howe to get back north in time to take New York. He was already overdue.

The British had expended 34,000 pounds of gunpowder in the futile siege of Charleston; the Americans, 4,766.[23]

It was emphatically an American victory, and all Charleston, all the colonies, applauded. Moultrie was made a general, and the fort was renamed for him. A battery there was named after Sergeant Jasper, who was offered a commission in the Continental Army. He declined the commission, giving as his reason his lack of education. He was illiterate.

The political repercussions were far-reaching. No Loyalist in either of the Carolinas was to dare to show his face out of doors for a long while. Continental enlistments leaped. That year of 1776, the first full year of the war, had ended badly for the Patriots in Canada and in the middle colonies, but it had ended with a rosy glow in the Deep South.

In England there were snarls and recriminations. Admiral Parker and General Clinton privately began to blame each other for what everybody admitted had been a fiasco. Through friends Clinton got Lord Germain to sign a statement that it had been none of Clinton's fault; but he was angry when Germain refused to consent to the publication of the statement, and even more angry when Admiral Parker started to spew his own ideas in print. Clinton, purple, got a leave of absence from his superior officer, Howe, and went back to England. It was widely believed that he carried a case of dueling pistols with him and that he meant to call Lord Germain out. Germain, never one to welcome danger, held him off with an Order of the Bath, so that the indignant one became Major General *Sir* Henry Clinton, K.C.B. This of course made General Howe furious; and hasty arrangements were made to give *him* a Bath as well. It was all very unfortunate.

CHAPTER

6

Pistols in the Morning

GEORGIA WAS HAVING TROUBLES of her own. Not only was she the youngest and least populous of the colonies, as well as the one farthest from Philadelphia, where the Continental Congress met, but she had also two frontiers to watch.

The Creeks, most numerous as they were the most warlike of the overmountain Indians, poised a permanent threat for the settlers of Georgia. Like the Cherokee, the Catawba, the Chickasaw, the Creeks had lost none of their ferocity, none of their fondness for slow torture, for scalps, but they *had* lost a great many of their skills. They no longer could make and use bows and arrows, and so were helpless to feed themselves unless they were supplied with lead and gunpowder by either the Spaniards to the west and south or the English to the east. The English had agents specially appointed for this purpose, and most of these agents, just out, were staunchly Loyalist in their local political opinions. The Georgians did not like them anymore than they liked the Creeks, or, for that matter, the Spaniards. They did not trust them.

The second frontier was to the south. It was barren and

unproductive, a sandy waste, but it could cause trouble, and as soon as hostilities with the mother country began, it did so. It was Florida.

The peace that ended the French and Indian War (the Seven Years' War) in 1763 provided among other things that Havana be returned by the British to the Spaniards, who for their part would hand over both of the Floridas to Great Britain, which held them anyway by right of conquest.

East Florida was the peninsula, the north-and-south Florida; West Florida was the rest, the panhandle.[24]

Britain had done something, not much, to populate the dreary place; but there were no minerals; there was precious little timber; the land was not fertile; and it was difficult to persuade Anglo-Saxons to settle in such a climate. Little, too, was done to improve the harbors at Mobile and Pensacola and St. Augustine, these being easily outshone by New Orleans on the one side and Charleston on the other. West Florida remained largely the domain of the Creeks, while East Florida contained only a few white indigo planters and livestock raisers clustered in the countryside around St. Augustine.

St. Augustine itself, the capital, was a tiny town. It was also a military post, the only one in East Florida. The garrison was a small one and in itself not capable of mounting an invasion of Georgia to the north, but it was commanded by Lieutenant Colonel Augustine (a coincidence) Prevost, a Swiss soldier of fortune who early petitioned General Howe and soon afterward General Clinton in New York for reinforcements that would enable him to organize just such a movement. In other words, Florida to the south was an ever-present threat.

It was worse than that. Some of its more spirited citizens, impelled no doubt more by hope of loot than by patriotic fervor, organized the Florida Rangers, a mobile, semimilitary body devoted to border raids, to cattle stealing. (The name

Rangers, denoting guerrilla fighters, was popular at the time, probably because of the éclat Rogers' Rangers had won in the French and Indian War. In the south the Rangers, unlike Rogers' men, were usually, though not necessarily, mounted; but they could not be considered cavalry.) These were obnoxious to the Georgians.

Also, St. Augustine had become a haven for the Loyalists of Georgia. It had become an escape hatch.

The southernmost colony in revolt—there never had been any thought of Florida joining the movement for independence—had almost no ties with its neighbors to the south, whose trade was largely with the West Indies or directly with the home country, but it did have close ties with the residents of South Carolina. It was only natural, then, that Georgia, though in no hurry to do so, should ally herself to the rebels.

Georgia had a royal governor, Sir James Wright, who was a decided cut above the royal governors in the other southern colonies; but even so, and though they treated him with some show of respect, the local Whigs were strong enough to frighten him into taking refuge on yet another British warship, this one the *Scarborough*, off Savannah. After that, they went to work on less exalted Tories.[25]

John Stuart was a man of middle age, Scottish by birth, a resident of America, and the king's representative among the southern Indians, a post he had held successfully for a long time. His heart was in his work, and above all he wanted to avoid the horrors of out-and-out border warfare. When the Whigs of Georgia seized what was meant to be a whole year's supply of gunpowder for the Creek nation, Stuart interposed vehemently. Didn't they realize, he cried, that gunpowder had become an absolute necessity to the overmountain Indians and that they would starve without it—or else go on the warpath? The Patriots brushed him aside; but they muttered something about his Loyalism as they did so, and Stuart, alarmed, escaped to the safety of St. Augustine.

John Hopkins was a mariner who one night in his cups held forth on what he thought of this new independence movement, and even went so far as to drink "Damnation to America." A committee called upon him next day and treated him to a hot-tar party. Hopkins, afterward, when he could move again, took ship to New York.

Thomas Brown was not so lucky. He had fled from Augusta, Georgia, to New Richmond, South Carolina, but the Sons of Liberty of Augusta went right after him, and took him back to that town, where they tarred and feathered him so severely that the man could not even walk for six months. And when he *could* walk, where did he go? He went to Florida. He lurked in St. Augustine, where he could be joined by his many friends.

This was the sort of thing that was happening all the while.

The Continental Congress on February 27, 1776, had created a Southern Military District, General Charles Lee's first independent command. After Lee had smashed the siege of Charleston, he returned north, hailed everywhere as a conquering hero. His place was taken by the North Carolinian Robert Howe, a major general now, and Howe was instructed, among other things, to help the Georgians in their laudable effort to stamp out that hotbed of Toryism, St. Augustine.

The Georgians already had taken steps toward this end. The trouble was, they could not get along with one another. They were a scrappy lot. Already two Whig parties were making themselves manifest. There was the radical, or popular or country, party, and there was the conservative party, city men mostly, merchants. (The "city" was Savannah, population 2,000.) Head of the one was Button Gwinnett; of the other, Lachlan McIntosh. These two—McIntosh was of Scottish extraction, Gwinnett was from Gloucestershire—never could get along.

Acting without any opposition—for the Tories were keeping their heads down—the Whig factions had got together long enough to adopt a suggested constitution, which provided for the election of a president of the state, in effect a governor. Archibald Bulloch, a good man, was elected to this post, and when he died suddenly late in February of 1777 he was succeeded by Button Gwinnett.

Now, Gwinnett was ambitious, and he fancied himself as a soldier. Nobody in Georgia just then had had any military experience, and he might have made as good a leader of the militia as anybody else, for he thought himself entitled to this position by reason of his presidency. The Committee of Safety did not agree; and when plans were made to reorganize the militia in preparation for a descent upon St. Augustine, the committee decreed that Lachlan McIntosh should be the colonel.

Gwinnett was furious. He caused the arrest of McIntosh's younger brother George on a charge of treason, accusing him of having sold rice to the Floridians, who were, after all, the enemy. (George McIntosh later was to be acquitted, but at the time it looked as though there might be some truth in the charge.) More, when the expedition at last was ready to go, Gwinnett insisted upon going with it, asserting again that his authority as president of the state entitled him to the command.

Prevost, a competent soldier, had made all his preparations, for everything that was done in Savannah was reported in St. Augustine mere hours later; but unless his reinforcements from New York arrived in time—and they didn't—he had no chance of holding St. Augustine with his token force.

The expedition never got there. It did round up a little livestock to take home, but it did not even threaten the capital of East Florida, and it inflicted no military damage upon that colony. The reason was that it fell apart. With two men giving orders, nobody knew whom to obey. The Committee of Safety at last called back both Gwinnett and McIntosh, leaving the command to the lieutenant colonel, Samuel Elbert; but by that time the damage had been done.

Early in May 1777, the new constitution officially went into effect, and Gwinnett failed to be elected to the permanent presidency. This failure probably was due to his mishandling of the St. Augustine expedition, but he blamed it on Lachlan McIntosh, who certainly had campaigned against him.

The legislature heard the case against Gwinnett in the matter of the George McIntosh accusation, and decided that he had behaved correctly. This enraged Lachlan McIntosh, who right then and there, on the floor, denounced Button Gwinnett as "a scoundrel and a lying rascal."

There was only one thing for a gentleman to do then, and Gwinnett did it. That very night he sat down and wrote a letter, which his friend George Wells, a member of the Assembly, took to the house of Colonel McIntosh, where McIntosh's friend, Major Joseph Habersham, was waiting to receive it.

This was a very high-toned affair, with everybody "sir"-ing everybody else, and the details were quickly and quietly arranged.

The men met the next morning, just before dawn. It was muggy, sticky. It would be a very hot day.

They were in a meadow behind Colonel Martin's house on the outskirts of Savannah. The land actually was owned by Sir James Wright, the royal governor, who had some time since returned to England, and since it was certain to be confiscated and sold to aid the rebel cause it was already as good as public property.

Everybody bowed. The principals looked properly casual. The pistols were McIntosh's, but they were acceptable to Gwinnett's representative. They were carefully loaded, carefully cocked. The distance, ten paces, was measured off.

There was only one fire. McIntosh, nicked in the thigh, was jolted, but he kept his feet. Gwinnett went down.

He had been hit in the right leg, just above the knee. It was a painful wound, but it did not look dangerous. He was carried off the field, and lay for three days in a fever. They were very hot days. Gangrene set in. On the third day he died.[26]

CHAPTER

7

The Weakest Link

THE WIZARDS OF WHITEHALL grew tired of trying to squeeze a colonial "waist." Gentleman Johnny Burgoyne, floundering in the wilderness between Lake George and the upper reaches of the Hudson, had been cut off from all his supplies and obliged to surrender his army, a deed that decided France to join the war. Howe, who had been meant to march north and make connection with Burgoyne somewhere in the vicinity of Albany, instead had gone south to the banks of the Brandywine, where Washington tried in vain to stop him. Howe did nothing more after that than occupy Philadelphia, which did him no more good than Boston had done him earlier in the contest. That is, he did not try to separate the American colonies by overrunning the Chesapeake region, as many had hoped he would do. He was recalled, and General Clinton, who succeeded him, was ordered to evacuate Philadelphia and concentrate in New York. Because of reports that a great French war fleet was approaching the

American side of the Atlantic, Clinton chose to make the trip by land. Washington's men, actually cocky as a result of that long, terrible winter at Valley Forge, intercepted him at Monmouth Court House, New Jersey.

It was June 28, 1778, the hottest day on record in that part of the world, and the sun laid out almost as many on both sides as did the muskets. The British casualties slightly exceeded those of the Americans, and the Americans kept the field; but though the reason for the fight was to prevent the British from getting back to New York, they got there, virtually intact.

Monmouth could be called a standoff or it could be called a British victory. In any event it was the last battle of the Revolution to be fought north of the Mason-Dixon Line. All the rest were in the South.

Still mindful that a chain is no stronger than its weakest link, the Whitehall thinkers proposed to roll up one of the enemy flanks, a time-tested tactic.

Maine? No! A brilliant young American colonel, Benedict Arnold, early in the war had penetrated Maine to invade Canada, but that had been an irregular move, not the planned, organized, properly conducted movement that Whitehall had in mind. And Arnold had been—Arnold. No, Maine was out of the question.

At the other end of the line, then, was Georgia. It was decided to invade Georgia.

It was possible to campaign the year round in that country. The British had good connections with the Creek Indians, whose very presence on the western frontier could tie up large numbers of Georgia settlers. The colony was the weakest of the thirteen in rebellion; it had the smallest population; and it was in serious financial difficulties. Also—and despite the violence and determination of the Whigs—the home government had reason to believe that there were still many Georgians who were Loyalists at heart and who would rally round the flag once that flag was shown. The ex-governors and the various other deposed royal officials were constantly assuring them of this.

It was impressed upon the British Commissioners for Restoring Peace in America—one of the members of which, *ex officio,* was General Clinton—that the most persuasive methods possible were to be used on the erring rebels, who were to be admitted once more under the king's protection with almost no qualifications, all the past being forgiven. Sir James Wright was to be sent back, together with a lieutenant governor. Only such force as was really needed should be applied, and as often as possible local Loyalist troops should be assigned to exert it.

Clinton in New York formed the invading force, which was to meet General Prevost (he had been promoted) at or near Savannah. Lieutenant Colonel Archibald Campbell was to be in command, and the force consisted of two battalions of his own regiment, the 71st Scottish; two Hessian regiments, the Woellwarths and the Wissenbachs; four battalions of assorted New York Loyalist volunteers, and a detachment of royal artillery, something like 3,500 men in all.

Savannah, a settlement of about 450 houses, was located on a high bluff. Once it had been fortified, but the fortifications had fallen to pieces. Still, it should have been easily defended, for it was hemmed in by swamps.

The Continental Congress had just appointed a new commander of the Southern District, the third, Benjamin Lincoln, an enormously fat Massachusetts farmer, who, however, was noted for his energy. Lincoln was still on his way south. When the British came, the defense of Savannah was in the hands of young Major General Robert Howe.

The descent could hardly have been a surprise. The Patriot spies at St. Augustine were not nearly so many or so able as the Loyalist spies at Savannah, but surely Prevost's

GENERAL BENJAMIN LINCOLN

preparations must have been reported. The expedition Campbell commanded was accompanied by a large fleet of war vessels under Commodore Hyde Parker, and when it started from New York late in November it had been driven back by bad weather and stayed several days for refitting. Surely its destination could be deduced? If it had been meant for Charleston, it would have been about twice as big.

Nevertheless Howe, hastily summoned, had the scantiest sort of reception plan. Campbell, all unopposed, landed his men on Tybee Island at the mouth of the Savannah River, about fifteen miles below the capital. Howe himself had inspected that spot, one of the few desirable landing places near Savannah, only the previous day; but he had left no entrenchments there, no guard, not even a nominal one.

There was a narrow causeway between rice fields to Girardeau's plantation house and the main road to Savannah, and this Howe *had* posted; but the British regulars easily drove in his pickets.

Beyond the plantation Howe had established his real defensive position. Bodies of Georgia and South Carolina militia were drawn up on either side of the narrow road, each with a fieldpiece of its own, each with a swamp protecting its flank. There were two fieldpieces mounted on the road itself, and a trench had been dug clear across from one swamp to the other.

This called for a frontal attack, which would be expensive. Campbell paused.

Then somebody brought forward an old Negro named Quamino Dolly, who said that there was a secret way through the swamp by means of which these determined men could be circumvented and the town reached without harm. He offered to guide them, and they gladly accepted his offer.

There was indeed a secret way, around to the right, and Dolly knew it. General Howe must have known of it too, but he failed to guard it, no doubt because he assumed that the way would *stay* secret.

Campbell feinted on his left, and then went around the other wing, to appear suddenly from behind. There was consternation in the American ranks, and many fled without even firing a shot, only to become lost in the swamps or swept away in the swollen streams. It wasn't really a battle at all: it was a rout. It did not last long. The Americans lost 83 dead and 453 captured; the British, 3 killed, 10 wounded. The British got, in addition, 48 cannons, 23 mortars, 94 barrels of gunpowder, and the capital.

The Patriots were in confusion, and Campbell was quick

to press his advantage. He marched up the river, on the west bank, and took Augusta without any opposition. It seemed almost too good to be true; and it was.

Prevost, delayed, arrived from East Florida, and a picked British force under the command of his brother, Lieutenant Colonel James Mark Prevost, smashed and scattered a Patriot militia force encamped on Briar Creek near where it empties into the Savannah. That was March 3. The very next day a civil government was proclaimed, a government to be headed by Colonel Prevost pending the arrival from England of the proper royal governor, Sir James Wright. As they had been instructed to do, the military men turned over to local civilians, to tried-and-true Loyalists, as much of the actual power as could be spared.

The plan seemed to be working well. Resistance was scattered, sporadic. Tories were coming in from the backcountry, coming down from South Carolina as well, though not perhaps in as large numbers as had been hoped. Hundreds took the oath of fidelity to George III every day. Thousands.

Nevertheless the Patriots had not been quashed. Everywhere they were on the move.

On February 14, Colonel Campbell, slightly alarmed by all the Patriot movement to the north and west of him, marched his forces out of Augusta, to settle a little farther south, nearer his base at Savannah. It was on that very same day that Andrew Pickens, John Dooly, and Elijah Clarke descended like a whirlwind upon Boyd's volunteer force of Loyalists encamped upon the banks of Kettle Creek—men who had intended to join Colonel Campbell and enlist as a body in the British Army—and scattered them, and captured their leaders, and tried these, hanging five.

It was the beginning of the really nasty part of the war.

The outliers began to come in, perhaps too soon. The

outliers were Loyalists who since Moore's Creek Bridge had not ventured to air their political opinions, much less to appear in arms for the king. In many cases they had literally slept away from home, at least whenever there were Patriot militia units in the vicinity. Now, eager to fight, hoping to get a chance to rob their Patriot neighbors even as their Patriot neighbors for so long had been robbing them, they were dismayed to learn that they were not warmly welcomed by the king's men, who indeed, and with good reason, distrusted them. Too often they were used, not as warriors, as they would have wished, but as laborers. In the towns and cities the Whigs twitted them about this:

> "Come, gentlemen Tories, firm, loyal and true,
> Here are axes and shovels and something to do!
> For the sake of your king,
> Come labor and sing."

In the backcountry of Georgia and the Carolinas, however, there was no twitting. Men there were in deadly earnest; and when outliers who had surfaced found that they were not treated with the respect they believed themselves to be entitled to, they had a tendency to desert: they would "lie out" again.

The Continental flank had not been turned, not yet, though much had been done to loosen it; and undeniably the acquisition of Savannah, that convenient port, was a great thing for the royal cause. Its recapture could make a world of difference in the war. The British knew this, and even in the first flush of their triumph they were making plans to strengthen the defenses of the capital against a possible counterattack.

That counterattack was to come, but in a form neither side expected.

Admiral-General Jean-Baptiste Charles Henri Hector

Théodat, Comte d'Estaing, was highly born, a true nobleman, and he was spirited and courageous, but his was not a career destined for immortality because of its military achievements. He had been a colonel in the French Army at sixteen, a brigadier general at twenty-seven, a promotion undoubtedly due rather to his blood lines than to his attainments. When the treaty of 1763 ended the Seven Years' War on terms humiliating to France, the whole official body of that nation devoted itself to the task of rebuilding the armed forces in order to be ready for the Next Time. D'Estaing then switched to the navy, possibly thinking that it offered a better chance for glory. Characteristically, he entered at the top, as a vice-admiral.

The world-shaking surrender of a whole British army at Saratoga in October of 1777 caused the French government to decide to help the American colonies in their struggle for independence—help them, that is, openly: she had already been helping them covertly. A huge fleet was assembled and equipped at Toulon, and the Comte d'Estaing was put in charge of it and was sent to America.

He took eighty-seven days in the crossing, and arrived off the capes of Delaware Bay just too late to bottle up the smaller fleet in command of Admiral Howe, who escaped in the direction of New York. D'Estaing pursued.

The Britishers rounded Sandy Hook and anchored in the bight between that spit and the "mainland" of New Jersey. The French halted just outside the Hook. D'Estaing had more vessels than Howe, and he had more guns, but the backbone of the French fleet, twelve enormous ships of the line, drew too much water for the bar between Sandy Hook and Staten Island. George Washington sent out the best pilots available, but it was no use; and after several days, doubtless cursing his luck, d'Estaing sailed north for Newport, Rhode Island, a British-held port that he and Washington had agreed should be the second point of attack.

Major General John Sullivan of New Hampshire was to meet him there and help to conduct a joint assault upon the British works.

Howe edged out of Raritan Bay and went into New York Bay, where almost immediately he was reinforced by four ships of the line and sundry attendant vessels in command of Admiral John ("Dirty Weather Jack") Byron.[27] Stronger, he made for Newport.

John Sullivan was a blunt country lawyer, and the Comte d'Estaing was no such thing, and they did not get along well together. After two days of disagreement, however, having accomplished nothing, they witnessed the arrival of the British. D'Estaing immediately reembarked his men and set sail, leaving Sullivan to do what he wanted about Newport.

For two days these fleets, like a couple of scowling, scared boys, circled each other. Then a storm blew up and scattered them both. Afterward Howe, shaken, was glad to make for New York, there to reassemble, while d'Estaing, refusing to go any further with the Newport project, sailed for Boston—for a long refitting.

The militiamen who had enlisted under Sullivan for the Newport campaign were deserting in droves, overcome with disgust. In Boston, too, there was a great deal of bitterness. So much had been expected of the French alliance!

D'Estaing discarded plans, never well formulated, for a Franco-American descent upon Nova Scotia, and instead went south to the West Indies, where he spent a few more months doing next to nothing.

It was at this point that Governor Rutledge and General (he too had been promoted) Moultrie, in South Carolina, heard of the French admiral's dilemma, and on nobody's authority combined to invite him to retake Savannah, as long as he was in that part of the world anyway.

The Weakest Link 65

There were two governments of Georgia just then, the royal one at Savannah, the rebel one in the backcountry, but neither was consulted.

D'Estaing gladly accepted the invitation. After all, he would have to go home soon and he wanted to do *something* first. He dropped anchors off Tybee Bar September 8, 1779. He had thirty-odd ships, besides his transports, and with the Negroes he had picked up in the West Indies [28] he had about 6,000 troops, most of them first-class, the cream of the French Army. The day before, he had stumbled upon a couple of British store ships and had taken a brigadier general and a £30,000 payroll intended for the troops at Savannah.

He could not possibly get across the bar with his deep-drawing warships, but he sent men and guns ashore by the thousands.

Prevost, even when he called in all his far-flung forces, had only about 2,000 men. The French alone had 3,500 regulars; and General Lincoln, who had been as much surprised as anybody else by the dramatic appearance of the French fleet, was bringing in a total of 1,350 Continentals and militia.

D'Estaing, paying almost no attention to Lincoln, called upon Prevost to surrender. Prevost asked for time to think it over, and d'Estaing, the fool, allowed it. Prevost was to use every minute of that time, day and night, building up the town's fortifications.

When finally pressed, Prevost reported that he thought he would fight it out; d'Estaing ordered his whole massive siege train to be brought ashore and set up. The French were thorough. They knew their business. But they had little faith in their allies, those clods; and to the elegant count-commander, Benjamin Lincoln—so fat, so earnest—must have seemed a clown.

The town was surrounded, except, of course, on the river side. It could not possibly survive. The French had everything—everything, that is, but time. It was already early October when the big guns began to cough.

D'Estaing's ships had no anchorage, no protection from wind or seas. The weather was beastly—rain, fog. Malaria was rampant. It had been many months since the sailors had been allotted fresh rations, and d'Estaing was losing thirty-five of them a day from scurvy alone. Worse, the hurricane season was near at hand.

Entrenchments were dug, many of them in swamps. Parallels were drawn. Guns were emplaced.

His engineers had assured d'Estaing that only ten days would be needed to take Savannah, but a serious shortage of draft animals made them extend this time. His captains, worried about their ships, were pleading with him to end the siege.

He did not wait the full ten days, but ordered a general attack.

The whole Irish brigade of the French Army, under General Dillon, got lost in Yamacraw Swamp and did not find their way out until it was too late to take any part in the fight, which was a fierce one.

Count Casimir Pulaski, an irascible volunteer from Poland, was hit in the groin by a musket ball, and toppled from his horse. His men quit the fray in order to bring him in; but he was to die, in agony, two days later.

Count d'Estaing himself was twice wounded, but he kept his feet.

The British were superb.

Only a few leaders of one outfit, the 2nd South Carolina Continentals, reached the enemy's fortifications, at Spring Hill Redoubt, near the center of the line. They planted their colors there, but they could not scale the redoubt itself in

COUNT CASIMIR PULASKI

the face of a murderous fire. The colors were shot down, and Sergeant Jasper, the same one, shinnied a pole to replace them; but this time he was killed.

It was too much for Admiral-General Comte d'Estaing. He called off the attack.

The allies had lost about 800 men, about 650 of them French. The British losses were trifling.

General Lincoln begged the count to stay for one more try, but d'Estaing had had enough. He limped back to France.

Lincoln, lacking cannons, could not retreat to Charleston, leaving Georgia wide open. The local Patriots, as the Bostonians had been, and the militiamen under Sullivan, were furious. What kind of help was *that?* they asked one

another. The Continental cause had never been so low, and the British were quick to take advantage of it. Within a few days after the end of the siege of Savannah, they were hawking pamphlets on the streets of that town:

> "To Charleston with fear
> The rebels repair;
> D'Estaing scampers back to his boats, sir;
> Each blaming the other,
> Each cursing his brother,
> And—may they cut each other's throats, sir." [29]

◄ THE ATTACK ON SAVANNAH

CHAPTER

8

If at First You Don't Succeed . . .

A FAMILIAR FIGURE in the military world is the officer who when he is in the lower ranks is all dash and bravura, full of daring ideas, but who as a commander becomes stiff with caution. Responsibility makes all the difference.

Such a one was Henry Clinton. Thin-skinned, testy, he had a talent for making enemies. Though as second-in-command he had been loud with helpful suggestions, when he got to the top he failed to look with favor upon any sign of original thinking among those beneath him. Now and then he could display a positively fatherly fondness for some promising aide, as he did for example in the case of Major André the spy, but more often he trusted no one, being convinced that the world was plotting against him.

Clinton was commander in chief now, and a careful man. As soon as he learned of Admiral d'Estaing's unsuccessful visit to the mouth of the Savannah, he determined —a rash move for him—to wrap up the Deep South while at the same time keeping firm his grip upon New York City and its environs.

The plan was not new. Clinton's predecessor, Howe,

had proposed it the previous year, but Lord Germain, the War Office, had said No at that time. Now, however, Germain approved the plan.

The first thing Clinton did was call in the 3,000 British regulars who had been occupying Newport, Rhode Island. What these men were doing there in the first place it is hard to see. True, they deprived the rebel privateers of the use of that port, which had been one of their favorites; but the Royal Navy was quite capable of doing that. Around headquarters in New York it was generally believed that Howe had ordered the occupation, which Clinton would lead, simply in order to get the man out from underfoot; and this could have been true.

George Washington, presently in New Jersey, was having all he could do to keep his ragged little Continental army intact, to keep it from disappearing altogether, but the now wary Clinton feared him all the same, living in daily dread of a thrust against New York City, which indeed Washington did seem to threaten. When at last Clinton set forth on his southern expedition, he left 15,000 troops in New York. These were in command of the highest-ranking German officer, Lieutenant General Wilhelm von Knyphausen.[30] Clinton's own second-in-command on the expedition was Lord Cornwallis, who carried in his wallet an unpublished "in America" commission as a lieutenant general. In view of the secrecy surrounding this commission, together with the fact that Clinton and Cornwallis were to quarrel bitterly about this southern expedition, there were many, even at the time, who assumed that Cornwallis was playing politics behind Clinton's back, hoping to supersede him. This was not true. Clinton knew about the unpublished commission, which was meant to keep a foreigner—in this case Knyphausen—from automatically becoming commander in chief in America, by reason of his rank, in case of the death or capture of General Clinton. These two were to find plenty of other things to squabble about. They did not need a secret commission to set them off.

The expedition cleared Sandy Hook the day after Christmas of 1779. There were 8,700 troops, besides 5,000 sailors and marines under Admiral Marriot Arbuthnot. They were in 10 warships and 90 transports.

They ran into weather trouble right away, and off Hatteras, already battered, they were badly mauled by the worst storm any of them ever had known. One transport, the *Anna,* carrying 200 Hessians, was blown clear across the Atlantic, to be wrecked on the coast of Cornwall. Virtually all the 396 horses, both artillery and cavalry, were lost: they had been carried in 18 of the transports, which barely survived. Many stores and much gunpowder also were lost.

They could not make directly for Charleston, as planned. They were obliged to put in at Savannah for a checkup and refitting first. They had been thirty-eight days at sea.

It was February 10 before the sails were seen outside Charleston harbor, and the day after that the redcoats began to disembark a little north of the city. The disembarkation was not opposed.

General Lincoln had about 3,600 men. These included the only Continentals south of Pennsylvania, but the force was made up largely of militia, all, of course, local. Other bodies of militia, from Virginia and North Carolina, were on their way. To these was to be added an irregular force of Charleston citizens who had been armed for the occasion. There were also large numbers of Negroes brought in from nearby plantations, but these were not armed—the thought of arming any Negro horrified the average Carolinian—but were used only as laborers.

It would not do. It was not enough. Nor could Lincoln hope for any reinforcements from Washington, who already was shorthanded.

If at First You Don't Succeed . . .

The lessons of the first attack had not been learned. The forts that were supposed to guard the entrance to the harbor, Moultrie (the former Sullivan) on the north, Johnson on the south, had been allowed to fall into virtual ruins. Johnson was not even garrisoned, and the 200-man garrison of Moultrie surrendered without firing a shot. Warships moved easily into the bay. Lord Rawdon arrived from New York with some 2,000 reinforcements, and these quickly sealed off any possible northern escape route by smashing the pitiful little force under Brigadier General Isaac Huger [31] at Monck's Corner.

Charleston, clearly, was doomed.

Clinton proceeded heavily, slowly, laboriously. He dug his parallels, and with the aid of sailors from the fleet he emplaced his big siege guns. There was no dash about him; he was a plodder; but he got there.

The only new idea in the siege of Charleston, attributed to the chief engineer, Major James Moncrieff, was in fact an adaptation of a very old idea. Moncrieff introduced the prefabricated mantelet.

The mantelet was a medieval device. It was—or it had been—a slanting platform of boards about seven feet high, propped up on the side away from the castle wall by means of a "leg" that was hinged to the platform. It was, in short, a portable breastwork. It was easily moved forward under fire of stones and arrows, and as easily moved from side to side or to the rear, the platform itself giving the archer protection, the "leg" being its handle. When the archer's arrow was in place, when he was ready to shoot, he could step out on either side of the mantelet, fire, and duck back.

The mantelet had not been employed in open battle, only in stationary siege warfare, and, like most medieval siege machines, was not carried with an army but improvised on the spot. Moncrieff, however, had caused *his* mantelets to be made in advance, in New York, for he had learned that there would not be much loose timber in the vicinity of Charleston.

Moncrieff's mantelets were 6 feet high and 14 feet long, and each was propped up by three "legs." It took eighteen men to emplace one of them, but these men were not archers, only diggers. The mantelets were used to protect the big guns. One could be set up before a gunsite in a matter of minutes, and then the eighteen men of the crew could quickly bank it on the outside, the enemy's side. The loose sandy nature of the soil in those parts made this task a notably easy one, and a safe one. Moncrieff's mantelets undoubtedly saved many lives; and the British before Charleston, though they were present in overwhelming numbers, never risked a single life unnecessarily.

Otherwise it was a very dull siege.

On April 10, when the first parallel was finished, Clinton and Arbuthnot sent Lincoln a summons to surrender. He declined. He might have *wished* to surrender, as the only sensible thing; but the political forces were too strong for him.

The South Carolina legislature in this crisis had voted to give the governor, John Rutledge, despotic power; and the lieutenant governor too, Christopher Gadsden, was an energetic if nonmilitary man. Gadsden was invited, or invited himself, to a council of war called by General Lincoln to discuss the possibilities of getting terms. He objected vehemently, and caused the meeting to be held over for one day. On the second day he produced a large number of what he called "witnesses," citizens of the town, who swore that they would defend it to the last man. One of these "witnesses" even threatened to shoot down the Continentals if they made any move to evacuate Charleston. There was nothing that Lincoln could do. He was the only Northerner present.

If at First You Don't Succeed ... 75

Despite the pressure, on April 21 Lincoln proposed an honors-of-war surrender. Clinton, sure of himself at last, refused.

The siege went noisily, thumpingly on. Charleston by this time was completely surrounded. And the big guns were getting nearer every day. They were slow, but as a giant is slow.

On May 8 there was another attempt to arrange a surrender. All that day and all the next day representatives of the two generals bickered beneath a flag of truce. Clinton was demanding a complete, unqualified surrender. He was rigid. He would not consent to any of the small, showy concessions so dear to the military heart. All colors must be handed in, furled. All arms must be laid down. The bands might not play either an English or an American air. This was considered very important, though it is not likely that in itself it was the cause of the breakdown of negotiations. For *that*, as is the custom in such cases, each side blamed the other.

That night, as though in a rage, all the guns on both sides opened up with everything they had. The sky was streaked with bursting shells. The earth shook. Men had to shout into each other's ears to make themselves heard.

This was kept up all night, without any pause.

It is possible that the Americans only sought to burn gunpowder that they would otherwise have to give to the British. Their shots were doing no harm, for the British were secure in their trenches and behind their breastworks. As for the British, they were using terror tactics pure and simple, scaring the populace, or what was left of it. They might have had some thought, too, of burning Charleston. Certainly they used some fire shells. Half a dozen houses were set ablaze.

Weak and worn, hollow-eyed, all fight gone, the citizens the next morning implored General Lincoln to call a halt, no matter what the terms; and this he did.

If at First You Don't Succeed . . . 77

About 6,000 men gave themselves up. This included some who were militia and some who were no more than armed citizens, but it included also the entire Continental military establishment in North Carolina, South Carolina, and Georgia.

It was the greatest blow that ever had been dealt to the new nation, and there were many who thought that it would prove fatal and that the war was as good as over.[32]

The British gained not only all these prisoners—though the armed citizens and the militiamen they set free, rather than feed them, on their vows not to take any further part in the rebellion—but also upward of 3,000 muskets, more than 33,000 rounds of small-arms ammunition, 376 barrels of gunpowder, 8,400 round shot, and the best port south of Philadelphia.

◄THE SIEGE OF CHARLESTON

CHAPTER

9

The All-American Murders

THE MOST HATED MAN in all the South was a short, stocky, cocky redhead with the improbable name of Banastre Tarleton. An Oxford graduate, son of the mayor of Liverpool, and as tough and rough a man as ever bestrode a horse, he had piled up a good record in New York and New Jersey under both Howe and Clinton, but it was not until he went to the Carolinas that he really bloomed. His name is remembered in those parts, even today, with hissings. "Barbarous Ban" was one of the milder things that the Patriots called him, though more often—and without a trace of affection—it was, simply, Benny. *He* wouldn't have cared what he was called, as long as he inspired fear, which he most certainly did. He had read for the law, but preferred the army. He had been in the service for five years and was a lieutenant colonel— at twenty-six.

He was a great one for getting things done. He had no patience with dillydalliers, shillyshalliers.

When Charleston fell, General Clinton's first move was

BANASTRE TARLETON

to send small fast bodies of redcoats out into the hinterland, in order to give the backcountry Loyalists rallying points, at the same time warning the rebels to keep under cover. There was no organized resistance, and in a very short time the British were the masters of South Carolina, which meant that they were also masters of sealed-off Georgia.

This called for cavalry, or at least dragoons, mounted infantry. The horses had been lost off Cape Hatteras, but this did not deter Banastre Tarleton, who took what he could get, the usual method being simply to seize the beast with the declaration that its owner was a rebel. Some of these were mere plow horses; but Tarleton, a born soldier, had a soldier's adaptability, and he made things do.

Sundry small groups of militiamen who had been on the way to Charleston when the news came of the fall of that city broke up and sought their separate ways home, to hide their muskets and to lie low for a little while. There was one comparatively large force, not militia, the 3rd Virginia Continentals, under Colonel Abraham Buford, to which this course was not open. There were about 350 of them when they ground to a halt about forty miles north of Charleston, having just learned that the intervening countryside was held by Clinton's men. When Charleston fell, a few days later, this was the only Continental group left anywhere in the South, and lest it be squashed so far from home Brigadier General Huger ordered it to turn around and march to Hillsborough, North Carolina, where he hoped to reassemble the scattered Patriot forces.

Buford started back. Clinton's second-in-command, Lord Cornwallis, went after him with more than 2,000 men. On May 27, however, at Nelson's Ferry, Cornwallis realized that he was never going to cut down on Buford's lead of more than a week, so he detached Tarleton's motley but fast-moving force to do so.

Tarleton at the time had 40 regular dragoons, 130 cavalrymen, and 100 infantrymen, who rode double behind the horsemen. It was furiously hot, but he drove them hard, as he always drove everybody, including himself. Horses began to drop dead; but Tarleton replaced them from farms along the way.

These men were not British. They were Americans, Loyalists, most of them New York and Pennsylvania militiamen.

They had ridden 105 miles in fifty-four hours, and their line was dangerously extended when, on the afternoon of May 29, they came upon Buford's rear guard. This was at a place called Waxhaws, near the North Carolina line.

Tarleton sent forward a flag, calling upon Buford to surrender. He had, Tarleton said, 700 men (he had barely 200 available), while Lord Cornwallis, just a few hours behind (actually two days' march), had nine battalions.

Buford considered for a little while, then sent back a refusal.

Tarleton immediately attacked. Any other commanding officer in those circumstances would have waited until all or most of his men were together, in order, and at least a little rested; but that was not Banastre Tarleton's way; he was a whirlwind.

The Virginians' rear guard was cut to pieces, and Tarleton's men charged on. The main body of the Continentals did not panic. Indeed, considering that they had never before faced a cavalry charge, they held their ground with commendable coolness, obeying their colonel's command not to shoot until the enemy was only about thirty yards away. That was too close. It may be that Buford had heard stories of the damage done at Breed's Hill by minutemen who waited until they saw the whites of the redcoats' eyes; but that had been infantry charging uphill, not horse on the level.³³ The volley at Waxhaws emptied some saddles, but it did not stop the charge, and before any reloading could be done the cavalrymen were in the midst of the Virginians, slashing wildly, right and left, with their long, razor-sharp sabers.

The infantry followed promptly, their bayonets fixed. The Virginians had no bayonets.

It was not a battle; it was a slaughter. Buford hoisted a white flag and called upon his men to down their arms, but the Loyalists paid no attention. They killed indiscriminately, often stabbing or slashing a man a dozen or more times where he lay. They even roamed the grounds in search of bodies with some slight twitch left in them, and they hacked those.

It was made even worse when early in the clash Tarleton's horse was shot under him and he disappeared from view. The word went out that he had been killed, and the Pennsylvania and New York men, shrieking in rage, set out to avenge him with their steel. Even when Tarleton got a fresh horse, it took him some time to call them out of their frenzy, for he was so short a man that he had to stand high in the stirrups to gain attention.

There is no evidence that Tarleton egged his men on to this savagery, but neither is there evidence that he did much to restrain them. He was not a man to be bothered by a little bloodletting.

The Virginians had lost 113 killed and 150 so badly wounded that they were left on the field to die. Fifty-three, most of them wounded, were taken prisoner. The Loyalist losses were 5 killed, 12 wounded.

After that, the phrase "Tarleton's quarter" had a special meaning. It meant no quarter at all.

The war in the South had its villain. It was all exceedingly personal. If Banastre Tarleton had chanced to be cap-

"Tarleton's Quarter!"

tured by any of the Patriot bands that still roamed through parts of South Carolina, there is no doubt of what would be done to him: he would be hanged. But he was too fast for that.

Clinton, when he returned to his headquarters, took about one-third of the total force with him, leaving Cornwallis six British regiments, one Hessian regiment, and six Tory regiments, about 8,300 rank and file in all.

Cornwallis's orders were specific. He was to stand on the defensive. The commander in chief had already established a line of strongly fortified places across the northern part of South Carolina, through Camden to Ninety Six, and this line, together with the seacoast line of Georgetown,

Charleston, Beaufort, and Savannah, Cornwallis was enjoined to maintain; but he was to leave any extension of it to his Loyalist allies, present and hoped for. This being perfectly understood, at least to his own satisfaction, General Clinton went back to New York.

Large numbers of surrendered muskets had been destroyed in Charleston immediately after the capitulation in an explosion caused when some, loaded, were carelessly piled. As usual, each side blamed the other; but it was probably the Britishers' fault, and they were understandably angry, for they had earmarked those guns for the use of the backcountry Loyalists. At about this same time, too, a rebel privateer had captured a British vessel loaded to the gunwales with muskets—probably army rejects—also meant for the Carolina and Georgia Loyalists.

They did not need to worry. The Tories of the hinterland had guns of their own, sometimes muskets, more often, near the frontier, rifles; and they knew how to use them. All they asked—and this the British cheerfully supplied—was a series of convenient forts or other strong points at which they could assemble and to which they could retreat for cover when whipped in the field.

For three months after the fall of Charleston there was bitter, harsh fighting in the backcountry. It was hard—even for them—to tell one side from the other. A few of the Tory outfits from the North, outfits characterized by staunchly Loyalistic names—the Queen's, the King's, the Prince of Wales', His Majesty's Loyal Legion, and the like—had uniforms. Most of them had none. It was tacitly arranged that the Loyalists would wear red rosettes in their hats, the Patriots green twigs. But hats could get lost in the fighting; and there were men who played it safe by carrying *both*, so that they could be sure of being on the winning side.

It was hit-and-run fighting, marked by a great deal of

house burning, a great deal of looting. Neither side seemed to be much interested in the redcoats, the Hessians, or the kilted Highlanders, who acted as garrison troops.

It was a horse-stealing war, a sentry-shooting sort of war.

Many of the fights—Ramsour's Mills, Rocky Mount, Winnsboro, Fishing Creek, Williamson's Plantation—were 100 percent American, or at most there might have been a sprinkling of British officers acting as advisers.

These were small if exceedingly bitter affrays. Hanging Rock, involving more than 1,000 men, could be called a battle. It lasted for four hours, and was very bloody, featured by a great deal of hand-to-hand fighting with clubbed muskets. The Patriots, as was so often the case, would have won an emphatic victory if they had only displayed a little discipline. Once ahead, they could not be kept together; and at Hanging Rock, when they broke into the Loyalist camp, and found a large supply of Jamaica rum among the stores, they almost threw their victory away, were almost cut to pieces by a counterattack.

Hanging Rock, though a first-class affair, settled nothing. Once again, it was all-American. There was not even a British "adviser" present. Today it is interesting largely because it was the place where a boy called Andrew Jackson got his first taste of warfare. He was on the Patriot side.

This kind of warfare called for a special kind of leader. The Loyalists, even the local ones, were under some sort of overall British Army discipline; and at least they could not change their officers at will, could not vote in a camp-meeting atmosphere what their next move would be, could not hold drumhead courts-martial. It was not so with the Patriots. Three of these stand out.

There was Andrew Pickens, a man in his upper thirties, of Scotch-Irish descent, a lean man of medium height, a

THOMAS SUMTER—THE "CAROLINA GAMECOCK"

taciturn man. It was he who had presided over the "war crimes" trial that followed the battle of Kettle Creek. When the British overran South Carolina after the fall of Charleston, Pickens surrendered a small fort near Ninety Six together with its garrison of three hundred Patriots, all of whom were released on parole. When, however, a little later, Tory troops looted his plantation on Long Cane Creek he announced that his parole no longer was valid, and he took the field again. He was a prodigious fighter. He was a farmer who had been a justice of the peace. He was an elder of the Presbyterian Church, and nobody had ever seen him smile.[34]

There was Thomas Sumter, who was to have a famous fort named after him. He was forty-one at this time, a rather short man, of English-Welsh extraction, and his men liked to call him the Carolina Gamecock. Like Pickens, he was given his parole after South Carolina was overrun, but when late in May of that same year his house near Stateburgh was burned by Loyalists under Banastre Tarleton he considered himself absolved of that oath and took the field again. He was a hammer-and-tongs type of fighter, who had little patience with the parade-ground formalities of army life. For all his violence, he was to live to be ninety-eight years old and to die in bed, the oldest surviving general of the war on either side.

There was Francis Marion, another small, taciturn fellow, forty-three years old, abstemious, of Huguenot stock. He was a Bible reader and the man the British most feared —for he was a masterful guerrilla, who could strike and then disappear almost before he had been seen. The British sometimes complained that he did not fight like a gentleman, but this never fretted him. His favorite lurking place was Snow's Island, which was not really an island at all but a low ridge five miles long and two miles wide, with the Pee Dee on the east, Lynch's River on the north, and Clarke's Creek on the south and west. Into this hideaway he would disappear after a strike, and there he and his men—they might number four or five or they might number four hundred or five hundred, for they came and went all the time—for months on end would live on sweet potatoes and swamp water laced with a little vinegar, or, when they were lucky, a snake or two. Tarleton himself, Barbarous Ban, once chased him, never getting a glimpse of him, for twenty-six miles through thick swampland, afterward exclaiming: "As for this damned old fox, the Devil himself could not catch him." This, it would seem, is how Francis Marion got his nickname, the Swamp Fox.[35]

This was the situation when the Continental Congress,

once again without consulting George Washington, who would have preferred Nathanael Greene for the job, appointed the hero of Saratoga, Major General Horatio Gates, to the command of the Southern Department. Gates started south to regularize the war there.

◄ FRANCIS MARION—THE "SWAMP FOX"—AND HIS MEN AFTER A RAID

CHAPTER

10

An Army of Scarecrows

HERE WAS NO KNIGHT in shining armor, no sitter on a prancing steed. Here was, rather, a fussy grandfather, a querulous, peevish, snobbish man, whose head habitually was thrust forward and who peered through thick-lensed glasses at those to whom he talked. He was the son of an English household servant—a very highly placed servant in a ducal household, to be sure, but a servant all the same. Doubtless through the influence of the duke (it was Leeds) he got a commission in the army, and rose to the rank of major. Beyond that he could not go. It had nothing to do with his capability or his record. He simply wasn't a gentleman.

He retired on half pay and went to America, a country he liked, for he had been with Braddock on the Monongahela and had taken part in the defense of Fort Herkimer. He bought and settled in the Shenandoah Valley, where he could move in the best society. In America he *was* a gentleman.

The Revolution opened new vistas for this ambitious middle-aged man. He and Charles Lee, another recent settler in Virginia, were the only Patriots with any sort of mentionable military background, and as such they were in demand. The man who had never expected to be more than a major suddenly found himself a major general.

In the beginning he was to prove an undistinguished though competent commander, but Saratoga made him. There was nothing brilliant about that campaign. Burgoyne, cut off from his base, having been denied a meeting with Howe from New York, floundered in a dense forest, surrounded by the Patriots, mostly militia, in overwhelming numbers, until at last, to save his men from starvation, he surrendered. But this was the first victory for the Patriots, and Gates was hailed as a genius, another Caesar, another Marlborough. Immediately there grew up in the Continental Congress—though to give him credit there is nothing to indicate that Gates, personally, did anything to encourage this—a movement to have him made commander in chief, replacing George Washington, who until that time had shown only a series of defeats. Nothing came of this movement; but Gates still was a popular hero when he was appointed to the command of the Southern Department.

His friend General Lee, who had once held that post, warned him against overconfidence. "Take care," he said, "lest your Northern laurels turn to Southern willows." Gates smiled this off. He was brimming with self-assurance when he started south.

He was preceded by Major General Baron de Kalb, a barge of a man, a professional soldier, born Hans Kalb, the son of a Bavarian peasant. He knew his business. As a boy, and using the name of Jean *de* Kalb,[36] he had joined the French Army, and since that time had seen plenty of action in Europe and in America. He was fifty-eight at this time. Though a good horseman, he still loved to walk, and thought nothing of thirty miles a day. He could sleep anywhere, at any time, under any conditions, yet wake up refreshed and

Major General Baron de Kalb

alert. His diet was Spartan, and he never drank wine or spirits.

Bits and pieces of the militia of North and South Carolina had been swept together by various underofficers, but it was a sad army de Kalb took over—discouraged, badly equipped, and, worst of all, hungry. He had brought with him several line regiments from Maryland and Delaware, not large units but reliable, the best in the whole Continental Army. These men, however, were so ill and weak that they could hardly walk. Dysentery had debilitated them. The quartermasters' organizations in Virginia and North Carolina, through which supplies must come, had completely broken down, and de Kalb and his Delawareans and Marylanders, together with a company of the Continental artillery, had to live off the countryside as they stumbled along.

It was green peaches and green apples for the most part, though now and then they would bring down a few of the lean cattle that roamed wild in the woods.

The Continentals, veterans of every action since the siege of Boston, had been expected to prove a rallying place for local militiamen, but the response had been anything but enthusiastic. Brigadier General Francis Marion did show up with twenty-odd men, so sleazy, so skinny, that even in that inelegant army they were greeted with derision. What was left of Count Pulaski's command, sixty horse and sixty foot, now under Colonel Charles Armand, joined the men from the North, but these too, once so gay, so spirited, were starving and in rags. Gamecock Sumter had been summoned, but as an officer of the South Carolina militia he did not have to take orders from General de Kalb, and he preferred to keep the field with his own command, for he never did work well with anybody else.

When they reached Buffalo Ford on the Deep River, in the very heart of North Carolina, they came to a stop. They couldn't go on, but neither could they go back. They were exhausted.

It was here that de Kalb heard of Gates's appointment.

This could hardly have come as a surprise. De Kalb surely had known that Congress would never keep a foreigner in command of the South while a real American was available. All he had to do now, until Gates came, was hold these sick, tick-bitten tatterdemalions together, and if possible increase their numbers. It would be a hard job and a thankless one, but he was used to jobs like that.

Gates arrived on July 25, a day of intense heat, and was saluted with thirteen guns, as became his rank. He had no doubts. He announced right away what he was about to do. He would attack Camden.

The strategy in itself was sound. Indeed, an attack upon Camden, in the very middle of the British line of fortified points, had been contemplated by de Kalb. But, that officer suggested, wouldn't it be better to take care of the men first, to feed them somehow? There would be plenty of forage where they were going, Gates replied.

By taking Camden, especially if it was taken by a surprise move, they could cut off the whole western portion of Cornwallis's perhaps overextended line. This then could be wrapped up, for Cornwallis on the coast would never dare to attack with the scanty forces at his command there. And of course such a move would be wonderful for morale.[37]

De Kalb and the others had reasoned the same way, but they proposed, when the men could be pulled together and in part cured and at least rested, to proceed to Camden by means of Salisbury and Charlotte, a western loop-around. This, including Rowan and Mecklenburg counties, was Patriot country. It was comparatively fertile. Crossing it, the men could get back some of their strength.

Gates said No. Gates said that they would go in a straight line. This would be some fifty miles shorter, but it would be through enemy territory, in effect, where they could expect no sort of food or supplies, and where the inhabitants, if any were left, would be against them.

Gates was the commander. They went by the direct route. It was a terrible trudge, during which the men often muttered of mutiny.[38]

They had lately been joined by a large body of North Carolina militiamen and a smaller body of Virginia militiamen, almost 4,000 altogether. These, however, were green troops. They had never been under fire. And they were that many more mouths to feed.

At the Pee Dee, as Gates had promised, they had come upon large fields of corn, which they ravaged. The corn still was green, and it made them sicker than ever.

Neither side was well served by its spies in this campaign. Gates seems not to have known that Cornwallis, having heard of his approach, had left Charleston, meaning to reinforce Lord Rawdon at Camden and to strengthen the middle of his line. Cornwallis, always a bold man, did this despite the fact that he had been misinformed as to Gates's strength. He believed Gates to have almost 7,000 troops, or two to three times the number he could possibly assemble in that place. Gates himself appeared to think, for a time, that he had that many; and when Colonel Otho Williams proved to him on paper, a series of reports from the field commanders, that he actually had only 3,052 present and fit for duty, Gates airily dismissed this by asserting that 3,052 "are enough for our purpose."

Lord Rawdon [39] had watched Gates's approach and had sent for his superior, who came from Charleston on the double. Rawdon led his small force out of Camden long enough to cause Gates to waver, to back a bit, and finally, on September 6, to encamp at Rugeley's Mill [40] on the Waxhaw road, about sixteen miles north of Camden. Cornwallis already had reached Camden.

Each commander that night decided to attack the other immediately—a night march, a dawn onset—and each started his army forward at about ten thirty. It was a narrow road, and a dark night.

The British made the faster time. They were better booted and better fed than the Patriots, and they stepped out briskly. The Patriots, on the other hand, were sick men. The redcoats and the Loyalists had had their prebattle tot of rum; the Patriots had not.

Rum was an accepted part of the rations of each army, but Gates was out of it, as he was out of so many things. He learned at the last minute, however, that there was plenty of molasses in the medical stores, so he ordered that this should be passed out, one gill to every man before the night march started. It was generally taken mixed with corn-meal mush, and the effect on gastrointestinal tracts strained by a diet of green corn and half-cooked meat—there had been no time to cook it properly—was appalling. Men kept falling out of ranks, tugging at the tops of their breeches as they did so. Some never found their way back in the darkness, and those who did were even further weakened.

Not only was it an army of scarecrows; it was an army of defecating scarecrows.

The British and the Loyalists had marched more than halfway to their goal, the rebels' supposed camp at Rugeley's Mill, and had just crossed Saunder's Creek, a shallow stream about two hundred feet wide, when the two advance guards, stumbling through the darkness, bumped into each other, to their mutual amazement.

There was some sharp firing, the bang of musketry sounding like the slamming of many doors. It was two o'clock in the morning.

Each side was uncertain whether it had collided head on with a mere scouting party or with the whole enemy army, and each sought to take a few prisoners. Both succeeded, and soon the shooting ceased, and the two commanders were being told what had happened, what had been learned.

Gage called a council of war, his first. Many of the officers, knowing the condition of the men, must have thought that a retreat would be the best course, but none of them dared to say so; and it was agreed that they should prepare for battle, which they did, deploying in the pre-dawn darkness.

Cornwallis was outnumbered, though not by nearly as much as he supposed: Gage had perhaps a 40 percent advantage over him. Cornwallis's troops, however, were veterans, and they included such crack outfits as the 71st Highlanders—the Black Watch. Gage's troops, always excepting the Delaware and Maryland contingents, were green-raw.

None of them had been under fire before. And the molasses was still having its effect.

The Patriots had perhaps a superior position, but their advantage was slight. The field was several hundred yards across, and lightly wooded. The Patriot position was a trifle higher, but such slope as there was could hardly be called a hill. Each side had its flanks protected by swampland. There would be no turning movement in the fight about to begin.

The Patriots, if they needed to retreat, had a clear course back to their baggage train, about halfway to Rugeley's Mill, but the British had Saunder's Creek behind them, which could prove awkward. Nevertheless, Cornwallis ordered a general advance as soon as the light allowed.

That light was not good. It was a foggy morning, and greasy gray strips of mist sauntered past the faces of the waiting men. The artillery pieces were posted forward of the first line on the road itself and on either side. These opened up early, and the smoke they caused hung in the air.

The first thing the Virginians on the extreme Patriot left knew, redcoated figures came racing out of the murk, their mouths open, their bayonets agleam.

The Virginians had bayonets, but these had been issued only the previous day, and not a militiaman knew what to do with his except that he had already learned that it made a good skewer if you could get any meat.

This was the first time the Virginians had ever seen an enemy soldier. They turned and ran. There were a few defiant shots, but most of the men made no pretense of resistance.

Tarleton's cavalry, which had been posted in the rear to be ready for just such an event, swept down upon the waverers, driving them into the swamps on either side or up the road toward Rugeley's Mill. Some of the latter paused at the supply wagons in order to see if they could find something to eat. They should not have done so. Tarleton's men were instantly upon them, with terrible results.

The rest of the Patriot left wing and center was made up of the North Carolina militia, some 2,000 strong. These men, seeing themselves unexpectedly exposed, did not even fire a few scattered shots. They just ran, many of them throwing away their guns as they did so.

In a matter of minutes the whole left wing and center had collapsed. They had disappeared.

Horatio Gates, who had stationed himself about two hundred yards behind the center, already was running. He had a fast horse, and he outstripped his own men.

The Patriot right wing consisted of the 2nd Maryland Continentals, under Colonel Mordecai Gist (the 1st Maryland Continentals under General Alexander Smallwood made up the second line, about four hundred yards behind, and they never did get into the battle), and the Delaware Continentals, under General de Kalb, who was in overall charge. If they had seen what happened beside them, they would undoubtedly have retreated, for they were good soldiers and would not have fought a hopeless fight simply in order to look like heroes; but because of the smoke they could not see, and they assumed that the militiamen were still struggling.

These right-wingers, about six hundred in number, soon were almost surrounded by a force almost twice their size. They fought on. They beat off two attacks and even counter-attacked once, taking some fifty prisoners.

The Baron de Kalb was everywhere among them. His horse had been killed under him, his head cruelly slashed by a saber, but he had no orders to retreat (Gates was too busy riding away to send such an order) and he seems never to have considered a surrender. When at last he fell, after almost an hour of the fiercest kind of fighting, he was bleeding from eleven places.

That took some of the heart out of the Marylanders and Delawareans, and soon afterward Tarleton's cavalry returned from the pursuit of the left wing and the center and plunged into their midst. Then, deprived of their leader, they fell back; but they never did panic.

The victory was complete. The Patriots had lost the field; and they had lost their colors, their guns, their supplies, and a very large percentage of their men, the rest being squandered over the countryside, especially in the swamps.

General Gates rode all the way to Charlotte, where he spent the night. Early the next morning he was in saddle again, and this time he did not draw rein until he had reached Hillsborough, 180 miles from the field of battle.

Hans Kalb, that tough old son of the soil, lived for three days.

CHAPTER

11

Toward the Chesapeake Squeeze

CHARLES CORNWALLIS, second Earl Cornwallis, was an honest man and straightforward. By no means arrogant or uppish, he was yet not one who liked to play second fiddle to anybody. Tall, urbane, he was in his middle forties. The only flaw in his strikingly handsome appearance was his left eye, which drooped a little, squinted a little. He could hardly see through that eye, the result of an accident on an Eton football field when he had collided with a lad who was later to become Bishop of Durham.

Cornwallis did not like the way his superior, Sir Henry Clinton, was running the war in America. Clinton simply sat in New York, like a frozen thing. From time to time he would make raids upon the surrounding countryside—New Jersey, Westchester County, Connecticut—and these raids, conducted in force, undoubtedly bit into the rebels' supplies, but in themselves they could not be decisive. Clinton's orders to Cornwallis, too, were to hold the line, to stand on the defensive. Seemingly the commander in chief was only hoping that the Continental armies, North and South, in time would simply fall apart. This was, of course, a possibility—several times a likelihood. But to Lord Cornwallis, always the man of action, sitting on one's bum was no way to win a war.

Cornwallis believed in the so-called Chesapeake Squeeze. He would have pushed up into North Carolina, and from there overrun Virginia, the most populous of the colonies and the one that produced not only great food supplies but also the most trade, trade in tobacco that served to keep the rebels in existence. With Virginia subjugated, he believed, the rebellion would be as good as finished.

He was not alone in this belief. So good a strategist as Benedict Arnold, who recently had done his flip-flop from the Continental to the British armies, believed, as he wrote to Lord Germain, that there were only two ways to end the war. One was by taking over the Hudson River for its entire length, splitting the rebellious colonies in half, and the other was by driving up from the South, through both Carolinas and Virginia and into the whole of the Chesapeake district. Either called for great force, concentrated force, and an end to the dispersion that the secretary of state, so far away, seemed to favor.

Arnold's morals left much to be desired, but he had more brains than all the other generals on both sides put together.

The traitor would have pushed north at least as far as Baltimore, farther if the occasion suggested it. Lord Cornwallis did not mention Baltimore in his letters to Lord Germain, but he did ask for permission to go beyond his orders from General Clinton by invading North Carolina and later Virginia, and Baltimore might have been in his mind.

There was nothing underhanded here. It was not even unethical. Clinton, before he sailed back to New York, had given Cornwallis permission to communicate directly with Lord Germain in London, instead of sending any such communications through the usual channels—that is, through headquarters at New York. This was done in the interest of time, because of the great distances involved.

Cornwallis took advantage of it, and he was soon convincing Germain, by letters, that the Chesapeake Squeeze was the best thing possible, the only sure thing. He had been instructed by his *immediate* superior to sit pat, not to venture out of Georgia and South Carolina, but soon he was being told by his *ultimate* superior, in Whitehall, to go ahead with such an invasion if he thought the plan feasible.

He had been prepared for this. He was gathering stores, seizing mounts, repairing wagons, training Loyalists. Like all the other British officers—with one notable exception—he had been disappointed in the response of "our people" in South Carolina and Georgia. They flocked in; they took the oath; but they were not reliable. Carefully led, and carefully watched by regular officers, they would fight as well as the next men; but there was no telling when they would desert, switch sides, often at the last, most perilous moment. Cornwallis hanged a few such deserters from time to time, but the others seemed incorrigible. He preferred to depend upon his own redcoats, or the Highlanders or the Hessians, men who knew how to obey orders.

The lone exception, the one British officer who had faith in the Loyalists, was Patrick Ferguson, a Scottish aristocrat, the son of a judge. He was a major, but held the "in America" rank of lieutenant colonel.[41]

Ferguson, a slim, thoughtful officer in his middle thirties, was reputed to be the best shot in the British Army. Many years ahead of his time, he had invented a breech-loading rifle. He had demonstrated this before high War Department officials, who were astounded at its accuracy and its long range; it could be fired six to seven times a minute, as compared with the two or three times of the standard British Army musket, the Brown Bess, and this with less likelihood of getting the powder wet; but it was never officially adopted, even on a small scale. There was a great deal of opposition to the rifle in the British Army, as there was to be in the American Army. Soldiers complained that it was dangerous in battle because a bayonet could not be affixed to it and also because it took so long to reload. It would carry two and a half times as far as a musket, and it was much more accurate, but the infantryman and his officers did not like it. The rifle might be all right for German Jägers, most of whom had been foresters before they were forced into the army;[42] it might be all right for certain light infantrymen on scouting duty; it might even be all right for those shaggy, buckskinned, long-haired frontiersmen who appeared now and then on the fringes of a proper force; but it would never do for a proper British soldier. Ferguson got nothing but "oh"s and "ah"s for his weapon.

A career soldier, in the army since his fourteenth birthday, Ferguson was not only a crack shot with rifle or pistol but also an expert fencer. When in the course of the battle of the Brandywine his right elbow was shattered by a musket ball, he did not lay aside these sports. He trained himself to shoot and even to fence with his left hand.

Cornwallis rode out of Camden on September 7, his army in three columns. The earl himself led the right wing up the east bank of the Wateree, while most of his cavalry and light infantry took the west bank, and the left wing, far out, was in command of Ferguson, who had about 1,100 men under him, all of them Loyalists. The idea was that by taking a wide western sweep Ferguson's Americans could enlist large numbers of their fellow countrymen as they went along, at the same time punishing with the torch recalcitrant rebels of the backcountry. Ferguson was confident that they could do so.

He let himself be led astray early in the march, when the commanding officer at the westernmost British post of

Ninety Six suggested that he try to head off Gamecock Sumter, who had just tried, unsuccessfully, to retake Augusta. Ferguson did not head off the Gamecock, but in trying to do so he got much farther west than had been planned. He and Cornwallis attempted to keep in touch with each other by means of mounted messengers, but they were in Whig territory now, where most of the men had rifles, and the messengers did not always get through.

Not because he enjoyed such tactics, as "Bloody Ban" Banastre seemed to do, but because he had been so instructed, Ferguson allowed his men to loot and then burn many houses belonging to Patriots. Understandably, he was not popular in that neighborhood. He even heard rumors that the weird, wild overmountain men on the western side of the hills had been alarmed by reports that reached them and were talking about organizing a force to attack him, Ferguson, and his assorted bloodthirsty Tories. To thwart any such movement among what in his own dispatches he always called the Back Water Men, he released a prisoner, Samuel Philips, and sent him west with a message for Isaac Shelby, a prominent Patriot leader, and for anyone else who cared to read it. He said that such talk must cease, for if it did not he himself would cross the mountains and hang the whole lot of them and burn their houses.

He should not have done that.

Cornwallis was having his troubles. When he moved the mass of his men in from the coast, he made the excuse that the interior would be less unhealthy than Savannah, Charleston, and the other towns. Yet on his way to Charlotte, North Carolina, his first immediate objective, his men were reporting to sick bay at an alarming rate. The weather was hot, and there was a great deal of malaria, as well as dysentery and cholera. It rained much of the time, making the ground sticky, the streams hard to cross.

It was September 22 before he reached Charlotte,

where none of "our people" declared themselves. Indeed, the populace was hostile, harassing his men, hiding supplies that he sought to seize. He was worried about Ferguson, who, the last he had heard from him, was about seventy miles away.

Then a messenger did get through from the backcountry, and the news he brought made Cornwallis reel.

His whole left wing had been wiped out.

He ordered a retreat.

CHAPTER

12

The Sword of the Lord and of Gideon

THE OVERMOUNTAIN MEN were frontier settlers who had found even the Carolina backcountry too tame and had gone down the west face to a land where the rivers all ran the other way, toward that vast, sprawling, mysterious region ruled by Spain. The toughest of the tough, they did not like to be threatened. When they heard about this man Ferguson and what he had said he would do, they decided to beat him to the punch.

There were some among them, like "Nolichucky Jack" Sevier,[43] for instance, who came from Huguenot stock; but most of them were of Scottish or Scotch-Irish ancestry, and when an emergency like this arose they had their own local equivalent of sending the flaming cross to all the remote glens. On the night of September 15, 1780, there gathered at Sycamore Shoals on the banks of the Watauga [44] more than 1,000 of these taciturn men, together with their horses and their womenfolk. Not all could cross the mountains in order to smite this man Ferguson hip and thigh, because the Creek and the Chickasaw could not be forgotten, but all could assemble to hear the send-off sermon, always the most important part of any campaign.

The Sword of the Lord and of Gideon

The Reverend Samuel Doak preached that sermon. He read to them from Judges, chapters 6 and 7, the story of Gideon, the son of Joash the Abiezrite, and how he was visited by an angel of the Lord, who demanded certain rather routine sacrifices in the name of the same Lord, while Gideon in return, to make sure that it *was* the Lord, demanded that certain minor miracles be performed to his satisfaction, and this was done. Doak told them how, under the guidance of the Lord, through that angel, Gideon, a man without any previous military experience, winnowed the original 32,000 Israelites down to an elite corps of three hundred, whom he armed with trumpets and lamps, the lamps being enclosed in pitchers. He told them how Gideon and the three hundred had fallen by night upon the great hordes of Midianites and Amalekites that infested the land of the Israelites like locusts, and had slain many thousands and caused all the rest to run so fast that they made straight shirttails. He told how the faithful three hundred then sought out the princes of the Midianites, Oreb and Zeeb, and hacked off their heads, to bear these back in triumph. Finally, he suggested that the warriors who were about to set forth adopt the same war cry that Gideon and *his* warriors had used on that memorable occasion, "The sword of the Lord and of Gideon." It was a little long, but such was the spirit of the meeting that it was unanimously chosen.

A few days later they started across the Blue Ridge, a ninety-mile trek, much of it in knee-deep snow.

They moved in two columns, one passing through Gillespie Gap, the other through McKinney's Gap, and they met five days later on Colonel Charles M. McDowell's plantation at Quaker Meadows,[45] where they allowed themselves some rest.

These men were all mounted. They carried rifles—the long "Kentucky" rifles—and they knew how to use them. They wore buckskin or linsey-woolsey, and they were a shaggy lot. Each carried his own rations, a bag or horn of parched corn sweetened with maple syrup or with honey. They could go for weeks with nothing else.

The countryside was in a turmoil, and no messenger's life was safe. Nevertheless, the overmountain men had managed to get word to certain leaders of the Virginia and North Carolina militia organizations, and now, east of the mountains, they were considerably reinforced. Colonel McDowell himself, who had conferred with them at Sycamore Shoals, reported that Colonel William Campbell was on his way with 400 Virginians and that Colonel Benjamin Cleveland and Major Joseph Winston would soon be on hand with some 350 North Carolinians. He had heard, too, that Colonel James Williams was trying to raise a force of South Carolina militia.

Ferguson, Colonel McDowell reported, was at Gilbert Town, a short distance to the south. Seemingly, he knew nothing of the overmountain movement, for he had not started to join his superior, Lord Cornwallis, at Charlotte; but surely he would hear of it soon.

The thing to do was catch Ferguson and smash him before he could make contact with the main British army. They could not hope to face the whole force.

They talked this over on October 1 and 2 at a gap of South Mountain near the headwaters of Cane Creek. It was raining.

They agreed to send their oldest officer, McDowell, to the Continental camp near Hillsboro and to ask for the services of an experienced military man, Brigadier General Daniel Morgan or Brigadier General William Davidson being suggested. Nothing came of this request. The overmountain men and their allies decided that it would not be safe to wait.

It was decided, informally, that the various colonels, Shelby, Sevier, Campbell, and Cleveland, should take turns in exercising the overall command, though it was tacitly agreed that the one with the most seniority, Campbell, would be in charge when the moment of truth arose. He was an enormously fat man, but energetic.

At Gilbert Town, not many miles to the south of them, Ferguson did hear of this strange mass movement. He must have been hard put to believe it. In his experience you didn't just raise an army out of nowhere, and in no time at all. An act like that requires a lot of preparation. All the same, Ferguson got out of Gilbert Town and headed south. Before he went he wrote to Cornwallis, who was laid up with a raging fever at Charlotte—though Ferguson did not know this—and reported the undeniable existence of this "ghost army," promising to rejoin his lordship soon.

A few hundred dragoons, he assured Cornwallis, could easily remove the new threat.

Whether Ferguson really meant to join his superior at Charlotte, or whether he planned first to go on south to Ninety Six, there to have another try at snaring the troublesome Sumter, we will never know. It seems certain at least that he hoped that his pursuers would think he was making for Ninety Six. After he had crossed the line into South Carolina, he swerved suddenly to the east.

The Patriots lost the trail for only a little while. There were many residents of that vicinity who were of their own way of thinking, and information was both plentiful and sound.

South of the state line the Patriots, too, turned sharply to the east. They halted that night at a place called the Cowpens. It was owned by a rich Tory named Hiram Saunders, and he had once used it as a place in which to herd his cattle, which were allowed to run wild for most of the year. If he actually had had pens there—enclosures, as seems likely—they were certainly there no longer after the Patriot army visited the place. Soldiers on the march are notoriously hard on rail fences, which make good campfires.

There, on October 6, in a heavy rain, they were reinforced yet again. The army now numbered about 1,790 men, all mounted but not all *well* mounted. A spy, one Joseph Kerr, brought the news that Ferguson, not far ahead, was occupying Kings Mountain. This could mean only that he had decided to make a stand.

Delighted, they agreed that he should not be given a chance to change his mind and to start on the double for Charlotte. They went over their mounts, picked the best, and told off about half of their whole force, a little over nine hundred men, to push ahead that very night, which they did. It was still raining. The men wrapped their flintlocks in blankets, in extra shirts, anything.

They rode all night. Once a party of Campbell's men got lost in the darkness, but soon after dawn they were recovered, and very little time had been lost.

They rode all the next morning. A few of the men begged for a rest, if only a short one, but Shelby, who was in charge, shook his head.

"I won't stop until night, if I have to follow Ferguson right into Cornwallis's lines," he said.

Ferguson, waiting for them, had about 1,100 men. One hundred of these were rangers, irregular regulars they might be called, picked partisans. The others were militia, equipped with muskets and with bayonets, in the use of which they had received some training. All were Americans. Patrick Ferguson himself was the only man on either side who was not an American.

Ferguson was known to be bold, but he was not thought to be rash. He seems on this occasion to have been negligent.[46]

In ordinary circumstances Kings Mountain would be an easy place to defend. But these were not ordinary circumstances. Ferguson at least seemed to think that he was safe, and he was said to have defied "God Almighty and all the rebels out of Hell" to dislodge him. He had ample supplies. In any event, there could be no thought of a siege. An army like the one he faced could not be held together long enough for a siege. Anyway, Cornwallis would soon send a relief column.

Kings Mountain is not a mountain at all; it is a plateau that forms one end of a series of hills called the Kings Mountain Range. It is about 500 yards long, and between 60 and 120 yards wide, and it stands about 60 feet above the surrounding plain. It is shaped like a gigantic human footprint, the toes northeast by east, the heel southwest by west. The top is level and bare, and Ferguson had done nothing to fortify it. Though the sides are steep, they are rocky and well wooded.

No outposts gave warning of the approach of the Patriots, who dismounted and tethered their horses about a mile from Kings Mountain. They formed into two columns of foot, and started forth immediately.

It was the middle of the afternoon, and these men had been on the march all the previous day, all the previous night, more than thirty-four hours in saddle; but they wasted no time. The rain had slacked to a drizzle. It was chilly.

They were within a few hundred yards of the base of the mountain before they were seen. They promptly surrounded it, and began to climb.

They moved in Indian fashion, from rock to rock, from tree to tree, shooting as they went, reloading, shooting again. As each group attained the top, Ferguson would order a bayonet charge. Before this, the attackers, having no bayonets of their own, would retreat; but they would not retreat far, and they kept shooting. This was the kind of warfare they knew best. They were at home here.

Three times they were pushed back. Three times they came zigzagging up again.

Campbell, waddling back and forth before his Virgin-

ians, constantly exhorted them to "shout like hell," which they did.[47]

The defenders, as so often happens when men shoot downhill, aimed too high. The attackers made every ball count.

Shelby and Campbell got there first. They took and held the southwestern end of the summit. The others followed soon after.

Ferguson, on a horse, tried to cut through Cleveland's line near the northeastern crest, the sole of the footprint, where the Loyalists had made their camp. Conspicuous with his right arm in a sling, he drew heavy fire, and was knocked out of his saddle, dead almost before he hit the earth.[48]

Captain Abraham de Peyster of New York took over the command, but there was not much for him to do except call for a surrender. The Loyalists now were completely surrounded, and many of them already had thrown down their muskets and were looking for something white to wave. More than a few were shot as they did so. This may have been in part because of a failure to hear the call for quarter in all that excitement, but it might also have been sheer savagery. Campbell's men in particular were in a rage. Their colonel had just been killed.

The battle lasted about an hour. The Loyalists had lost 157 killed outright, 163 so badly wounded that they were left on the field to die, and 698 prisoners. The Patriots had lost 28 killed, 62 wounded. It was still raining.

The Patriots spent that night on the field, and the next day—it was a Sunday—they started for home. They were afraid that Banastre Tarleton, who had been in charge of Cornwallis's second column, up the west bank of the Wateree, soon would be among them, slashing right and left with his great sword. They moved fast.

The Sword of the Lord and of Gideon

The prisoners were hard to corral, and they escaped in large batches. At last, a week after the fight, at Bickerstaff's plantation near Gilbert Town, North Carolina, the overmountain men staged a mass trial of those who remained.

Thirty were found guilty of war crimes, and these were condemned to death. Most of them were pardoned at the last moment. One escaped. Nine were hanged. There was only enough wood available to build three gallows, so they were hanged in groups.

After that, everybody went home.[49]

◄ PATRICK FERGUSON "WAS KNOCKED OUT OF HIS SADDLE, DEAD ALMOST BEFORE HE HIT THE EARTH."

CHAPTER

13

The Studious Blacksmith

It was an unceasing source of amusement to the Britishers that the officers among the rebels, even the general officers—in fact, it sometimes seemed as though it was *especially* true with the general officers—were not soldiers at all, only men playing at being soldiers. At home, of course, an officer in the army was always a gentleman in the first place, and his first commission was bought for him, usually while he was in his middle teens. The army to such a person was a full-time profession, a dedication, anything else being inconceivable. To these odd Americans it was only a game, a temporary thing, a condition. It was not their regular way of life, but an *interruption* to their regular way of life. The English thought it ridiculous that men in so many other prosaic professions and businesses, even in trade, should suddenly sew on epaulettes, strap on swords, and call themselves "generals." Thus, Weedon had been an innkeeper, Wayne a tanner, Muhlenberg a minister of the gospel; thus, Glover had been a fish dealer, Sullivan a lawyer, Arnold the proprietor of a chemist's shop. Preposterous!

Some thought of this might have been in Horatio Gates's

GENERAL NATHANAEL GREENE

mind on December 3, 1780, at Hillsborough, North Carolina, when he formally handed over the command of the Southern Department to Nathanael Greene of Rhode Island. For Gates, after all, was an Englishman, a full-time career soldier, who until just the other day had spent all his life in the British Army. And Greene was—a blacksmith.

Greene was a slow-smiling man, a trifle overweight but not really fat. He stood five foot ten and had broad shoulders. His sandy hair was turning gray prematurely—he was thirty-eight when he took over from Gates—and he had a high forehead, a florid complexion, and blue-gray eyes, the right one blemished after a faulty inoculation. He seldom raised his voice, and he never dragged his heels. He did not look like a soldier, nor did he move like one—he limped on his right leg, the result of a boyhood injury to the knee—but the making of anchors, his ordinary vocation, to him was always secondary to the militia, his real love. An omnivorous reader, though a monoglot, he had read everything pertaining to the military art in English or in translation that he could get his hands on, right back to and including the classics. He really studied these books, really pondered them. Because of this overriding interest in the army, he had been read out of the Society of Friends. No Quaker should be so bellicose—and let it show.

A leader in the Rhode Island militia, he had been one of the first to turn out after Lexington and Concord, so that now he had been five and a half years in active service. He had risen easily from lieutenant colonel to major general, but until this time he had never had an independent command. He had a small boy's absorption in the trappings of the military life—the flags, drums, parades—yet he also had a hardheaded regard for the facts of camp life—the dirty details, the drudgery. It was a curious combination.

George Washington, no mean judge of men, had great faith in Nathanael Greene; and indeed Greene's only enemies, military enemies—for he had no other kind, everybody liked him *personally*—were those who feared that he had too much influence over the commander in chief. It was Washington who had nominated him to be the head of the Southern Department, when Congress after the crashing loss at Camden at last had appealed to the commander in chief for advice.

It is notable that Greene was instructed specifically to take orders from the commander in chief. Practically, this was of little importance, for George Washington would not have thought of imposing restrictions upon a field commander so far away, and Greene to all intents and purposes was on his own. But it marked a decided rise in Washington's prestige. The previous commanders of the Southern Department—Howe, Lee, Lincoln, Gates—all had reported to and taken their orders from the Continental Congress.

What Horatio Gates thought about this we do not know,

The Studious Blacksmith 119

but to the amazement of everybody around headquarters the two got along very well indeed. Greene had been instructed to bring Gates before a court-martial that would look into his dispositions and behavior at and immediately after the Battle of Camden. Gates himself sought such a court, but Greene told Congress that it could not be mounted in the field because he did not have another major general, having left Steuben in Virginia to expedite the shipping of supplies. So, there was no cause for friction between the two.[50] In the short time that elapsed between the arrival of Greene and the departure of Gates, they were infallibly polite to each other in public and, it would seem, on excellent terms in private.

Greene knew what a mess he was inheriting. Even before he left Philadelphia he was raising supplies, writing ahead to governors and to the leaders of militia. His efforts were largely fruitless. Maryland and Virginia, and now North Carolina, had worries of their own. Most of the officials sympathized with Greene, and wished that they could do more for the Continental cause, but this was not always true. The governor of Virginia, for instance, lank, redheaded Thomas Jefferson, was ready with only eighteen of the one hundred wagons General Greene had asked for; and he did not seem to regret it. In truth, Jefferson struck Greene as a strange sort of man, actually more interested in the rights of the citizens of Virginia than in the needs of the soldiers, an attitude Nathanael found hard to understand.

At Hillsborough, Greene took over from Gates 90 cavalrymen, 60 artillerists, and, on paper, 2,307 infantry. Actually, there were only 1,482 infantry well and present, only 949 of them Continentals, and fewer than 800 of them properly clothed and equipped.

Major General Alexander Leslie, it was reliably reported, was on his way from New York with 2,500 troops, most of them regulars, to reinforce Cornwallis.

France by this time was unmistakably, irrevocably in the

war. After several false starts she had at last landed an army at Newport, with a fleet to protect its overseas communications. This, many British officers believed, meant that the rebellion could never be fully put down. Still, if something could be saved—Georgia, the Carolinas, Virginia maybe, even Maryland—the rebels' teetering organization could not be expected to have a long life. With Canada on the north, and these conquered colonies on the south, whatever new nation might emerge in the middle would be, to say the least, a dangerously weak nation. Thus went realistic thinking in certain high British Army circles.

There was no reason to believe, however, that Charles Cornwallis subscribed to this belief. Though he had sympathized with the legitimate political complaints of the colonists, he was first of all a soldier, and rebellion he could not abide. The war could yet be won, he believed, and he meant to win it.

George Washington had not been able to spare his friend many troops when the transfer was made, but the ones he did let go were thrillers. Lieutenant Colonel Henry ("Light-Horse Harry") Lee, of Virginia, a Princeton man,[51] had a handpicked legion of almost three hundred men, about half of them mounted, half on foot. They were something to see and to cheer as they jangled into the miserable little Continental camp. They wore tight-fitting green coats (like Tarleton's men), steel helmets with plumes, and white leather breeches. Among those daymares, tossed about in that sea of inconcinnity, they must have caused many a caught-up breath.

All the color, therefore, was not on the side of the British. There was a cavalry outfit in the Carolinas when Greene got there that for sheer dash could caracole with anything led by Banastre Tarleton or the gifted young John Graves Simcoe, commander of the Queen's Rangers, another Loyalist group. This was Lieutenant Colonel William Washington's company

COLONEL WILLIAM WASHINGTON

of dragoons, about a hundred of them. They wore white coats and, again, steel helmets. Their leader, a six-footer with broad shoulders and long arms, had been studying for the ministry when war broke out, but he took to fighting like a duck to water. At Trenton, under his second cousin once removed, the commander in chief, he was one of the two Continental officers (young Lieutenant James Monroe was the other) who were wounded. *That* was only a nick in the hand, but he was badly hit in the course of the fighting on Long Island. Nothing stopped him; nothing daunted him. His superiors sometimes complained that he was inclined to be too free and easy with his men, which did not make for good discipline, but in the field he was fearless—and very fast—and he could swing a saber with the best of them.

Greene had, too, the services of Tadeusz Andrzej Bona-

BRIGADIER GENERAL KOSCIUSZKO

wentura Kosciuszko, one of the few good military engineers in America. He was a hard man to get along with, but he knew his business. He had the brevetted rank of brigadier general.

It was Greene's idea that the many rivers in the district were not being used to their full military capacity. He set his Polish subordinate to work surveying these rivers and devising a sort of wooden platform that could be mounted on wheels and used as a wagon on land or taken off those wheels and used as a raft on the water.

At Hillsborough, Greene and his men were in a countryside that had been stripped of all its foodstuffs. He simply could not stay there. He proposed to split his skimpy little army in half.

Here was military madness, the pundits would say. To divide your force at any time was bad enough, but to divide it in the presence of a superior enemy force was esteemed little less than suicidal. Nevertheless Nathanael Greene did so. The men, he realized, must eat. And he believed that Lord Cornwallis, who had retreated to Winnsboro, South Carolina, would not move again until Leslie arrived with the reinforcements.

A prodigious worker, Greene already had reorganized his army from top to bottom, appointing a new quartermaster general, a new commissary general, a wagon master, a forage master, a clothier general, a commissary of prisoners, and a commissary of hides. This last was to take care of all the hides that the camp butchers had left, and see to it that they were somehow converted into shoes. Large numbers of the men still were walking around on bare feet.

Greene also kept up a correspondence with personages in the north, most of it requests for materials or for money. He was forever ordering camp kettles and horseshoes, flints and flutes, shirts and stockings.

"A new lord, new laws," the old saying went. Militiamen had a habit of quitting the camp with or without official leave, and returning anytime they pleased. The new commanding officer soon put a stop to this practice. He took the first such returnee and hanged him out of hand, publicly.

Greene, then, defying all the rules of warfare, took about half of his men, some 1,100 of them, part Continental, part militia, to a "camp of repose"—his own words for it—at Cheraw Hill. He sent the rest, 320 Maryland and Delaware Continentals, 200 Virginia riflemen, and Washington's white-coated company, to cross the Catawba and operate between the Broad and the Pacolet rivers after joining up with North Carolina militia outfits under General Davidson and Major Joseph McDowell.

The two divisions were about 140 miles apart, with many a high-running river between; but Greene reckoned that if the western one was threatened, he himself—he stayed with the Cheraw Hill division—could threaten Charleston: he was

BRIGADIER GENERAL DAN MORGAN

actually a little nearer to Charleston than Cornwallis was at Winnsboro. On the other hand, if *he* was threatened the western division could either fall upon Camden and Ninety Six, at the western end of the British line, or else fall upon the western flank or upon the rear of the attacking British army. And *each* division would be in country where food supplies were comparatively plentiful. Moreover, it had not been necessary for either to look as if it were retreating in order to get to that desirable location.

The western division was turned over to the command of a newly made brigadier general, a former wagon driver. This was Daniel Morgan of Virginia.

He was a large rawboned man of Welsh extraction, as the name indicates. He had had little formal education, but was by no means illiterate, and was a natural leader of men.

He had been known in his time—he was now in his upper forties and ailing—as the fastest man with his fists up and down the whole frontier. All wagoners were rough, and Daniel Morgan was the king of them.

His military experience was scanty. He had driven a supply wagon under the ill-fated General Braddock, along with many another hired civilian, one of them a young fellow named Daniel Boone. Yet when the Revolution broke out, he had signed up right away, and marched from Virginia to Massachusetts at the head of a noisy passel of riflemen. They had been rather troublesome volunteers, those frontiersmen from Virginia and Maryland, crack shots but bad for discipline, always fighting among themselves, and Washington had been glad to send many of them, including Morgan, out of the camp at Cambridge with Benedict Arnold to invade Canada.

Morgan had performed prodigies of valor on that expedition, and a little later was to prove his merit again in the campaign against Burgoyne. Nevertheless, Congress had passed him by when it came to promotion, allowing him to remain a mere colonel, while lesser men, nincompoops, were made brigadiers. Daniel Morgan had quite properly resigned.

But when his own state of Virginia had been threatened from the south, he had made his peace with the Continental Congress, had been promoted at last, and had gone off to join Gates, later to be transferred to Greene, who put him in charge of the western division of his army.

Morgan certainly was not the rough-and-tumble fighter he once had been. He was stiff with rheumatism now, had a touch of sciatica, and a malarial hangover, and also, as he wrote to Greene, suffered from piles. The men loved him. They called him Old Wagoner.

Lord Cornwallis had been greatly perturbed by the unorthodox splitting of the rebel army. He had too much respect for Nathanael Greene to lay it to ignorance, and he smelled a trick. Yet this was clearly his time to take the offensive. He had about 4,000 well-equipped troops, most of them regulars, but even his Loyalist volunteers, Tarleton's legion and Simcoe's legion, were armed with British weapons, trained by British sergeants, led by British officers. Greene had barely 3,000 men, more than half of them raw militia, all of them badly clothed, all of them hungry.

After mature deliberation Cornwallis split up his army into *three* divisions, One, under Leslie, he left to guard Charleston and the other coastal points, and also to maintain the Camden–Ninety Six line. Another, under Tarleton, he sent west of the Catawba with orders to pursue and destroy Morgan's force. He repeated the phrase "and destroy." He might have saved himself the trouble. You didn't need to tell a man like Tarleton a thing like that twice.

The major part of the army he kept under his own command. He was still determined to invade North Carolina. His previous attempt had been spoiled by the wholly unexpected battle of Kings Mountain, but it was clear that nothing like Kings Mountain could ever occur again. In North Carolina he would be in a good position to intercept and to stamp out any remnants of Morgan's smashed force that had escaped Tarleton to the south. After that, Tarleton could rejoin him, and together they would go into Virginia, at the same time cutting Greene's Virginia–North Carolina supply line.

Braced, then, he started forth. For the second time he invaded North Carolina.

Then all hell broke loose behind him, and once again he had to order a retreat.

CHAPTER

14

He Turned with a Snarl

IF THERE WAS ONE THING that the Old Wagoner hated, it was to have somebody snapping at his heels. Banastre Tarleton was carrying out orders with his customary spirit, so close upon Morgan that for two nights his men had slept among the still-warm campfires of the Continentals. It looked as if Morgan might soon be pushed over the Broad River, which would take him into the Kings Mountain region, where, if things went according to plan, Cornwallis would be waiting for him. Morgan refused to oblige. Five miles short of the Broad was a district known as the Cowpens, the very place where the overmountain men had paused in the pouring rain to take on more militia before pushing ahead to Kings Mountain and the defeat of Ferguson; and it was here that Daniel Morgan turned with a snarl.

He was to be severely criticized for doing so, and even at the time, his officers expostulated with him. A worse place for a battle, in the circumstances, they said, could not be found. This was a gently sloping plain, lightly wooded with pine, chestnut, and oak, with no undergrowth, virtually a park, a perfect stamping ground for cavalry—and Tarleton, only a few miles to the east, outnumbered the Patriots three to one in the matter of cavalry.

Morgan countered (or later said that he did) by expressing the belief that Tarleton would not even think of a flanking movement, but would come straight in, with his head down, as he always did.

There was no swampland nearby, the officers pointed out, and this meant that both flanks would be left "in the air"—that is, unprotected.

Most of his men were militia, Morgan retorted, and if they saw a swamp they would hide in it to get out of danger.

The Broad, which *was* broad in that season of rains, was at the Patriots' backs, the officers argued, and this would block any possible retreat.

Morgan answered that if he took his men across the Broad when the British were so close behind, he would lose half of his army from desertion then and there.

He may have thought of these things later, but it is likely that he considered them at the time.

There were two other reasons for stopping short of the Broad. One was forage. Morgan had written to Greene that he was desperately short of forage and might have to invade Georgia in order to get to some. This would have taken him even farther from his superior officer and into a correspondingly perilous position. The other reason was that the Cowpens not only had plenty of forage but would also make an ideal trysting place. There were various small bodies of militia wandering around the countryside in search of Morgan—in particular Andrew Pickens and his guerrillas. Morgan sent out word to make it the Cowpens.

In fact, Morgan was joined by Pickens and a force of militia that very night, the night he encamped at the Cowpens, January 16–17, 1781. There were probably not many of these, perhaps seventy or eighty, and Morgan had little faith in such raw troops, but the leader himself, the dour Presbyterian elder, was a mountain of strength.

Anyway, Morgan stopped. He had decided, for whatever reason, to cease running and to fight.

In numbers of men the two sides were about even. Tarleton had his own Legion of 550, half horse and half foot, all Americans; one battalion, or 200 men, of the 7th regiment of the line (the Royal Fusiliers); the 1st battalion, about 200 men, of the 71st Highlanders (Fraser's); 50 members of the 17th Light Dragoons, and a small detachment of Royal Artillery, about 1,100 in all. He had also some local Loyalists, but these probably were acting only as guides. He had two 3-pounders, horse-drawn guns mounted on high leglike sticks, so that they were called "grasshoppers"; but these played no part in the battle.

Morgan had no artillery. His best troops were the western Continentals from Maryland and Delaware, 200 riflemen from the western part of Virginia, and Washington's 80 dragoons, but he also had General Davidson's 140 North Carolina militiamen, Major Jacob McDowell's 200 South Carolina and Georgia riflemen, and 30 mounted infantrymen from South Carolina and Georgia, about 1,040 in all. To these must be added the men Pickens brought in at the last minute.

Among these men, as they cooked their dinner on the night of January 16, at the same time cooking breakfast in advance—for the general wanted them to fight on full stomachs—the Old Wagoner passed. He joshed them, told them stories, teased them about their sweethearts back home. For all his rheumatism and his other ailments he seemed perfectly at ease. He always referred to Tarleton as Ben or Benny, which somehow made the man seem less fearful than the more customary Bloody Ban or Barbarous Ban. It was said by some that the Old Wagoner more than once peeled off his shirt and showed the soldiers the stripes on his back— stripes put there by a British Army sergeant with a cat-o'-nine-tails when Morgan was serving under Braddock in the Pennsylvania wilderness, one hundred "of the best" for having knocked down an officer who cursed his mother. This could be true. It was the sort of thing he *would* do.

Moreover, he saw to it that his whole plan of battle was explained not only to the officers but to all the men. It was different from anything they had ever heard before.

The first line would be the weakest, consisting of the newly joined North Carolina men under Pickens. Morgan assumed that these men would run away, but he wanted to make sure that they got off a couple of shots apiece before they did so. They were instructed to this effect. They were to shoot twice, at a distance of no more than fifty yards, and *then* they were to run back to the second line, where room would be made for them.

The second line was made up largely of South Carolina militia, who had similar instructions: fire twice, aiming carefully, then retreat. Together with Pickens's men they were to run back around the main line's left wing. There was a slight rise of ground there, and behind this they could pull themselves together, get back into line, reload, and return to the battle by means of the Patriots' *right* wing, acting as a reserve.

The main line, made up of the Continentals and the Virginia riflemen, most of whom were former Continentals and therefore veterans, was not to run away. It was to stand.

Behind yet another rise of ground, directly back of the American middle, Washington's dragoons and Lieutenant Colonel James McCall's forty-five mounted infantry from Georgia were to hold themselves in readiness to throw themselves into a surprise attack wherever and whenever this seemed called for. The Georgia men were armed with sabers so that they could fight from the saddle.

The Patriot troops, then, turned in early after dinner, unworried about the morrow, knowing that a good breakfast was waiting for them. It was not so with the British. They had put in a heavy day of marching, but they were to be rooted out of their blankets not long after midnight, and sent forth again. For four hours they trudged through mud that they could scarcely see. They were cold, and their stomachs were empty, but Tarleton, obsessed by the idea that Morgan might yet get across the Broad, drove them on.

Dawn was to be a little after six o'clock, sunrise almost an hour later. The great part of the British force by that time was across Thicketty Creek, and Tarleton had learned from his advance scouts, who had clashed with the Patriots' pickets, that what he had most hoped for had come true: Morgan was making a stand. Tarleton might have rested his men a bit then, and given them a chance to get breakfast, for no one was threatening his position; but he was a very importunate young man, and he ordered a charge right away. He was a slam-bang sort of fighter; and, just as Morgan had foreseen, he did not spend time reconnoitering, feeling out the enemy flanks, but drove furiously ahead.

He did send out a screen of fifty dragoons. Only thirty-five of these came back, and they were shaken men who could not be induced to take any further part in the fighting.

Unfazed, Tarleton ordered a full advance, keeping only Fraser's Highlanders (the 71st) as a reserve and some two hundred of his own Legion horsemen.

The first Patriot line, the North Carolina and Georgia riflemen, did exactly as they had been told. They got off two careful shots and then fell back to the second line, a distance of about 150 yards. There was no hint of panic. They reloaded as they went.

The musketeers, their bayonets fixed, came on at a trot, yelling. Pickens's men, reinforced by the militiamen of the original first line, fired steadily and well, not by volleys, as was the British Army system, but each man for himself. As often as possible, they picked out epaulettes and fired between them.

The oncoming line wavered, but straightened itself and charged again.

Unruffled, the Patriots filed off to the left of their own line, loading as they went, sometimes pausing to shoot. Those farthest over on the right of this line had the greatest distance to go, and for a little while they were, or seemed, unprotected. Tarleton ordered forward the 71st Highlanders, who went in with a skirl of pipes.

At that moment, and seemingly from nowhere, there swept into sight Washington's white-coated dragoons and Colonel McCall's mounted Georgia infantrymen, their sabers flashing. The British right, astonished, reeled back. It was as though a whole new army had sprung up out of the ground.

The third line, the Continentals and the Virginia riflemen, had been ordered to stand their place, and this they did. The Highlanders got almost within bayoneting distance of them, but the long-shooting rifles, coolly handled, prevailed. Then, too, William Washington, having driven back the British right wing, slashed his way across the field to fall upon the British *left;* and at the same time the first two lines of militiamen, having reorganized behind the protection of the little hill, came on the run around the Patriots' right, to fall, in their turn, upon the Highlanders.

The artillerists refused to give up their pieces—or themselves. They were cut down almost to a man.

The British right and center had been broken into small parties, most of them desperately anxious to get away. Many men threw down their muskets and pleaded for quarter. "We'll give you quarter," the Patriots shouted, *"Tarleton's quarter!"* It was all that their officers could do to avert a massacre.

The Highlanders held together, and fought on until almost the entire Patriot force was against them and all around them, and even then they surrendered only on terms. They kept their colors, and when their commanding officer, a Major McArthur, handed his sword to Colonel Pickens—who was soon to be made a brigadier for his part in the battle—it was promptly and courteously returned.

WILLIAM WASHINGTON AND BANASTRE TARLETON AT COWPENS—
"FACE TO FACE, ONLY A FEW YARDS APART, EACH WITH A SABER IN
HIS FIST. . . ."

Tarleton, who could scarcely believe his eyes, rode to the rear to bring up the rest of the reserve, the two hundred dragoons who had taken no part in the fighting. They were fresh, and all the rebels had been in the fray for almost an hour. But the dragoons would have no part of it. They defied their master to his face, and wheeled about and rode off. A few miles back they came upon the baggage train, and saw that the panic had reached even there. The redcoats left to guard the train were hastily unhitching the horses, and mounting them, to ride away.

Tarleton rode after the dragoons, and Washington, who saw him go, rode after *him*.

The two were to meet face to face, only a few yards apart, each with a saber in his fist, and for a moment it looked as though there might be a between-the-lines duel of champions in the old knights-in-armor tradition. This was not to be, however. Tarleton drew a pistol, and fired, missing Washington but wounding his horse, and then rode on.

It was the last shot of the battle.

The Patriots had lost 12 killed, 60 wounded. The British had lost 100 killed, 229 wounded, all of them prisoners, and 600 nonwounded prisoners, nearly nine-tenths of their whole force. In addition there fell to Morgan's men 100 horses, 35 wagons, the 2 grasshoppers, 800 muskets, the colors of the 7th regiment, a traveling forge, and all the enemy's musical instruments.

Also taken were some 60 Negro slaves. These were officers' servants, not field hands. The field slaves that they could seize from any Whig planters the British habitually shipped to the West Indies for sale, for they rated them as legitimate spoils of war.

The Revolution had put on a new face.

Cornwallis was to exonerate his adjutant of all blame,[52] but, explain it as he would, he must have known that his plan to invade North Carolina and Virginia had ground to a halt.

CHAPTER

15

What Is a Victory?

THERE WAS ANARCHY in the Deep South. Attempts on both sides to set up some kind of civilian rule had failed. The British had established a series of forts or fortified places from Charleston to Augusta, but these were no more than combined police stations and military warehouses, and no man, be he Patriot or Loyalist, was safe half a dozen miles from their walls. There were ten of these forts, most of them in South Carolina, none at all in North Carolina.

The bitterness was unabated. Compared with what happened in those parts, the war in New England, New Jersey, Pennsylvania, was a polite business, a patterned business. In the beginning it had been thought enough to threaten a political enemy with a flogging or a tarring, perhaps now and then to carry out such a threat; but as hatred deepened, recourse was had to hangings. Both sides hanged men out of hand, without any pretense of trial. Sometimes the men who did so had some kind of militia membership; but often they were out-and-out desperadoes. Politics was an excuse, not a motivation.

Prisoners were beaten or killed in cold blood. Houses were stripped of their furniture and then burned.

There was horse stealing everywhere. The distances were great, supplies uncertain, and the need for speed so pronounced in that broken-up country that the planter or farmer who had been visited by the soldiery was lucky if he was left even his oxen, much less his horses, which might be formally commandeered but more often were just taken. Though much of the hanging was based on horse stealing, hanging was practiced freely by both sides.

Sumter the Gamecock and Marion the Swamp Fox often had to wait in hiding for weeks on end while they gathered enough men to make a series of raids practical. These were never long sorties, never campaigns. As soon as the men could accumulate as much loot as they could carry, they lost interest and would go home, and Marion and Sumter would have it to do all over again. There were Sumters and Marions among the Loyalists as well. They are not known to fame, in part because they did not have such colorful nicknames, but mostly because their side, in the long run, lost. Nevertheless, they were there.

There are some battles—and the '80 and '81 campaigns in the Deep South were rich with them—that can be called victories by both sides. Nobody ever has given a valid definition of victory on the field of battle. Is the winner the army that loses the less? Or takes the more prisoners? Or keeps the field? Or attains its original purpose—even though that purpose was a negative one?

This was not true of the Cowpens, a clear-cut victory, a smasher. Yet the Cowpens did not get Daniel Morgan out of danger. Cornwallis was not far away, and he was coming fast. On the very afternoon of the battle the Old Wagoner moved his men across the Broad, and after that he would have gone even farther west, right into the hills, had not Greene, hearing of the plan, forbidden it. The Old Wagoner was miffed, but he obeyed.

Greene had sent his heavy baggage to Guilford Courthouse, a pleasant little village near the center of North Carolina, and it was there that he united the two divisions, Morgan's and that of Isaac Huger, February 9.

It occurred to Greene that Guilford would make an excellent place for a battle, and with this in mind he examined it and its environs thoroughly, making notes. Not that he thought of a stand against Cornwallis then! He was too weak for that, having fewer than 1,600 men, and those half naked, half frozen, half starved, while Cornwallis had about 3,000. Greene did, however, call a council of war. A man who was always willing to listen to advice, though he seldom commented on it, he appeared to have little use for the institution of the council of war, an institution much favored by George Washington. Perhaps Greene thought such councils a waste of time. Anyway, he did call one at Guilford Courthouse.

It was at once agreed that no stand could be made against Cornwallis with the army as weak as it was. It would be necessary to back clear into Virginia before reinforcements could be expected. Furthermore, Virginia was rich in food supplies, though Von Steuben's efforts to dispatch these to Greene's army in the Carolinas repeatedly were spoiled by raiding parties sent out by Major General William Phillips, who had recently succeeded Benedict Arnold as commander of a task force sent to Virginia to take some of the pressure off Cornwallis. Very little had been getting through to Nathanael Greene, who sometimes wondered aloud whether Congress had not decided to ditch the Deep South. (In fact, there was a party in the Continental Congress in favor of doing that very thing. Georgia and the Carolinas, many thought, were a drag. The appointment of Greene to the command of the Southern Department was looked upon as one last try.)

The question was, What would Cornwallis do? Recently, at a place called Ramsour's Mill, North Carolina, he had caused all his heavy supplies to be burned or otherwise destroyed, first tossing to the flames his own personal effects. He had even caused the rum supply to be poured out. Clearly his purpose was disencumbrance. He wished to be able to move faster, which made it look as though he meant to chase and catch up with and smash to bits Greene's shaky little force.

Or, Cornwallis, who already had a healthy respect for his American opposite number, might have reasoned that Greene surely would have gathered all the boats on the Dan in advance, to ensure his passage across the river that at that point divided Virginia from North Carolina. Greene had in fact done so; and Cornwallis might suppose that to beat him to the Dan would be impossible. In that case his lordship might head for the upper reaches of the Dan, where there were fords that could be used to cross the river without boats. This would take him farther from a junction with Phillips's army, farther from Greene's men, who would then be given a chance to recuperate and to recruit, and farther from his base, already almost two hundred miles away. Still, he might be desperate. He was certainly not a man for halfway measures.

Alternately, the British commander might swing suddenly to the left and penetrate deep into Virginia, all the way to Charlottesville, in the very shadow of the Blue Ridge, where he could rescue and attach to himself the convention army, a prize indeed.

This so-called "convention army" was the force that Burgoyne had surrendered to Gates at Saratoga three and a half years earlier. According to the convention signed at that time, the men should all be shipped back to Great Britain with the understanding that they would not be used any further in the war. On technicalities, on one excuse or another, the Continental Congress had failed to do so; and the army was still in durance. It had been kept for about a year at various places near Boston and at Rutland, Massachusetts, and then had marched for twelve terrible weeks in

What Is a Victory? 139

January and February to Charlottesville, Virginia, where it still was. Originally it had consisted of 4,991 officers and men —2,139 British, 2,022 Germans, 830 Canadians. It had not been well guarded, and escapes had been frequent, especially on the march through Pennsylvania, where so many of the Hessians had dropped out to take refuge among German-speaking farmers. There had been deaths, too. At Charlottesville there might be only about half of the original army; but that still was a good bag. Additionally, the prisoners taken at the Cowpens, some 800 of them, had been sent to Charlottesville.

A messenger was dispatched to warn the stockade authorities at Charlottesville, but it was the consensus of the council that Lord Cornwallis would make directly for Greene's army with the idea of exterminating it, no less, and that the best thing for them to do was head for Virginia in a hurry. Greene, agreeing, told off some seven hundred of the lightest and fastest troops, including all the cavalry and mounted infantry, to act as a sort of retreating screen in the hope of making Cornwallis think at least for a little while that the main body was making for the fords of the upper Dan. The command of this fast-moving unit was offered to Daniel Morgan, but he begged off, for he said that his ailments were too much to permit him any action in the field, and he was allowed to resign and to betake himself, with his sciatica and his piles, to his own part of Virginia—the western part. The command then was given to Colonel Otho Holland Williams of Maryland, a man who had energy, imagination, charm, and a white horse named Liberty.

Thus was started what historians like to call, a shade breathlessly, the Race to the Dan. Nothing like it ever before had been known. Military men to this day go over every foot of that chase, a classic.

The distance from Guilford Courthouse to the Dan River, the Virginia line, is only seventy miles, but this was midwinter, the icy rains from time to time turning to snow, and in that Pine Barrens country the thick red mud was hub-high. Most of the men were barefoot. They had no tents, and there was only one blanket for every three, in some outfits every four.

Williams's rearguard men, often in sight of Cornwallis's van, never far from it, were allowed only one hot meal a day, only three hours of sleep out of every twenty-four.

The race was always close. Sometimes it was a matter of mere hours, sometimes, it seemed, of minutes.

Greene made it. On the morning of February 14 he got over his entire force, rearguard and all. Cornwallis was left on the south bank with no boats.

Cornwallis could not just stand there looking foolish. To scout the shore for boats possibly overlooked would be a waste of time: already Cornwallis knew his opponent well enough to shrug off that possibility. It was too late now to make for the fords of the upper river, and *much* too late for a dash in the direction of Charlottesville. His men had been razor-keen in the pursuit, but now they sagged with weariness, and many were ill. Nor did they have any more rum.

He fell back by easy stages to Hillsborough, North Carolina, in the very middle of the Loyalist country, and there he hoisted the royal standard and gave forth a plangent proclamation summoning all friends and faithful subjects of George III to come forward and enroll in the cause.

The response was not heartlifting. "Our people" flocked to see Lord Cornwallis, and they hurrahed him with gusto, but they did not join up. It seemed very strange. Had he or had he not chased the rebels clear out of South and North Carolina, not to mention Georgia? Did he or did he not command the only real army for a hundred miles around?

Then suddenly, early in March, "our people" ceased to come to camp at all, ceased even to cheer, but remained silently in their homes. And very soon Lord Cornwallis learned the reason, a reason that had reached the civilians by grapevine before official sources became aware of it.

Greene had recrossed the Dan. He was in the Carolinas again. He had taken up the position he previously favored, at Guilford Courthouse. He was waiting there for Lord Cornwallis.

Cornwallis did not disappoint him. As Greene had foreseen, the noble lord could not fail to accept such an invitation, no matter what the odds against him. Cornwallis was not a man to turn away from a fight.

They read each other well, these two. They were like fencers who face for the first time, when each knows, at the first delicate touch of the steel, that he is meeting a master. One rhymester, in a quatrain that was to become popular, compared it rather to a dance:

> "Cornwallis led a country dance,
> The like was never seen, sir,
> Much retrograde and much advance,
> And all with General Greene, sir."

Greene had enlisted many a Continental in Virginia, though most of these were raw, and he had upward of 4,000 soldiers altogether—some said as many as 4,500. Cornwallis, whose army had suffered much from illness and from desertion, had barely 2,000. This made no difference to Cornwallis, who had perfect confidence in his men.

Greene had learned the lessons of the Cowpens. He put his weakest militiamen in the first line, begging them to get off two shots before they fell back; his stronger militiamen and his new Continentals were in the second line; and the third line, which was expected to stand, was made up of his veteran Continentals. There were two divergencies from the Morgan plan. Morgan had set up his lines only about 150 yards apart, but Greene, probably because of differences in

What Is a Victory? 143

the land, made his almost twice that. Morgan had allowed himself no avenue of retreat, but Nathanael Greene was careful to provide such an avenue, though he could hope that it would never be used.

Cornwallis was not going to try anything new. He just sent his men in headlong, great masses of them.[53]

It was an exceedingly savage battle. The American militiamen did fall back, but they did not panic, nor did they throw away their guns. The British were magnificent. They proved once again—as if further proof had been needed!— that in a toe-to-toe slugfest they were the greatest fighters in the world.

It was touch and go for a while. But British ferocity at last prevailed, and Greene called for a retreat, which was conducted in an orderly manner.

The British kept the field, and therefore the British could be considered the victors, but they had paid a ghastly price. They lost 532 men, killed, wounded, and missing, which was 28 percent of their whole force. The American losses totaled 261.[54]

After Bunker Hill, this was the bloodiest battle of the war.

◄ "IT WAS AN EXCEEDINGLY SAVAGE BATTLE"—THE BATTLE OF GUILFORD COURTHOUSE

CHAPTER

16

The Big Wipe-Up

GREENE WON BY LOSING. "We fight, get beat, rise, and fight again," he wrote to a friend, the French ambassador. Nevertheless he had Cornwallis worried, though Cornwallis was ordinarily a sanguine man. Two days after the Battle of Guilford Courthouse, Cornwallis withdrew south, leaving the worst of his wounded behind. Nathanael Greene, full of bounce, went right after him.

Cornwallis proceeded painfully down the west bank of the Cape Fear River. He had hoped to rest his men there a little and to stock some food supplies from the Cross Creek country, where the Scots, though they had taken no part in the war since the fracas at Moore's Creek Bridge, still were Loyalist in their sympathies. This was not to be. The Scots had barely enough to eat for themselves, and small parties of rebels were cutting out supply wagons and boats, while Greene gave the redcoats no rest. It would seem that even to continue to exist Cornwallis must cross the Cape Fear River and march down the east bank to Wilmington, almost one hundred miles away. Such a crossing could be a perilous thing, and Cornwallis knew it—and Greene knew it, too.

Greene was in a position to pounce—a pounce that might well have ended the war in the South—when suddenly and unexpectedly half his army disappeared.

These were the North Carolina and Virginia militiamen so lately and laboriously enlisted. Greene knew that they had been signed up for only sixty days instead of the more customary ninety. What he had not known—and what he was to learn only at this critical juncture—was that they interpreted this agreement to run from the time of the actual signature until the time when each man walked back to his house and hung up his gun over the fireplace. By this measurement, when they had spent twenty-three days in the field they were free to quit. And quit they did.

The British then could make their crossing and totter down to the comparative safety of Wilmington, while Nathanael Greene, with a sigh, turned south.

Greene had about 2,600 men left, about 1,600 of them Continentals. Irregular forces under Sumter, Pickens, and Marion still were in the field, but they could not be counted upon. Even supposing that Cornwallis stayed in Wilmington instead of swinging south for the purpose of crushing Greene between two forces, his own and that of Lord Rawdon, Greene had less than a third of the number of men the British had under arms in Georgia and the Carolinas. However, the Britishers were stretched in strongpoints along the coast—Wilmington, Charleston, Savannah—and in forts and fortified places strung out to the westward, ten of them. Greene's obvious strategy was to descend upon these forts one by one and gobble them. He began with Camden, the strongest.[55]

He never got there. Rawdon, always pugnacious, went out to meet him. The resulting tussle is sometimes known as the Second Battle of Camden, but in truth it occurred several miles to the north of that town, a place called Hobkirk's Hill. It was a standoff, but the British could claim it as a victory because they held the field. Rawdon, however, soon afterward realized that he could not hope to maintain such a long line, and he left Camden, after burning his fortifications there. He did not yet know whether he could count on any help from Cornwallis, who was still at Wilmington.

Greene retired with his emaciated men to the High Hills of Santee, where at least they would be free of malaria. It promised to be a scorching summer. Lee's men and Captain Washington's continued to be on the move, cooperating from time to time with the partisans, and it was these, together with occasional groups of Continentals from the main body, that took the British fortified positions one by one. It was hard work, thankless work, and likely to be bloody, for the forts for the most part were defended by local Tories, some of whom had deserted from the Patriot forces, and who knew that they would be hanged if they were captured, and therefore fought fiercely.

Sometimes a frontal assault was made. Sometimes parallels were dug and guns brought up. On one occasion the defenders were induced to surrender without firing a shot by the promise that they would be given free conduct to Charleston with all the loot that they could carry.

Charleston, at its most unhealthy as summer crept in, was crammed with Loyalist refugees. Most of them were in a malodorous little suburb named—and the name was meant to be pejorative—Rawdontown. The Loyalists were not safe anywhere inland now, only in the ports.

The only thing new about this form of warfare was the "invention" of the so-called Maham Tower, attributed to Colonel Hezekiah Maham, a South Carolina man. This was first used in the successful siege of Fort Watson and later in the unsuccessful siege of Ninety Six. Maham had noted that most of the fortified places were only stockades, not blockhouses—that is, they had no roofs—and that in the absence of siege artillery, of which the Patriots in the Carolinas and Georgia had none, they could hold out indefinitely. So he sent men with axes into the nearby woods. It took him five days to assemble enough logs, only one day to build the tower itself, a square structure with a parapeted top slightly higher than the walls of the fort. It was a modern adaptation of the wooden fighting towers erected in large numbers outside medieval castles under siege; but it was hailed as a great discovery.

Ninety Six itself, the strongest fort of them all, was the last to hold out. The Patriots never did take it. Just as it was about to fall—and there surely would have been a massacre *there*—Rawdon appeared from Charleston with more than 2,000 regulars fresh-landed from Cork. However, after he had saved it, Rawdon decided to destroy and abandon Ninety Six anyway. It was too far out.

Cornwallis? He had reconnoitered the land between himself and his still-standing line between Charleston, Camden and Ninety Six, and found it unfavorable. It was bare and would provide no rations. What inhabitants it did have were known to harbor rebel sympathies. There were several unpredictable rivers, between any two of which Cornwallis and his men might be trapped by the ever-alert Nathanael Greene. Besides, Cornwallis was obsessed by the idea that he could win the war, crush the revolution, by marching into Virginia and joining General Phillips. And now Greene at least was out of his way.

On April 25, 1781, Cornwallis marched north from Wilmington. On May 14 he met Phillips near Petersburg. From there he turned east—toward Yorktown, where indeed he was to end the war, though not the way he had planned.

He was caught in a cul-de-sac, a fact that at first did not faze him, for he had confidence in the ability of the British Navy to get him out.

It happened, however, that this was one of those rare

occasions on which the British Navy did not hold the coast of North America with overwhelming superior forces. The French had a fleet under de Grasse in the West Indies, and this easily made its way north to and into Chesapeake Bay; and when on September 5 a British fleet arrived from New York to open an escape route for the entrapped Cornwallis, de Grasse sailed forth to meet it.

He sailed raggedly between the Virginia capes Charles and Henry, keeping a poor line, his van dangerously far ahead of his rear. If the British admiral had jumped him at that time he could have mauled him unmercifully, and almost certainly would have gained entrance to the bay and contact with Cornwallis. But the British admiral, Samuel Graves, was not ready. He was a man of conventional mind, and he would play the game as he had been taught.

Not until four o'clock that afternoon did the two fleets close, and by that time the French line had been straightened.

De Grasse had twenty-four ships, all of them big, all well gunned and well manned, one, the flagship, *Ville de Paris*, being the biggest vessel in the world.

The British had nineteen warships and four frigates.

The wind was from the north-northwest, which gave the British the weather gauge.

Until well after sundown they volleyed and thundered, close up; and then cautiously, panting, drew apart, each like a scared schoolboy hoping that the other would run away.

This was a turning point. It should have been one of the most decisive, one of the most dramatic sea battles in history, another Trafalgar, another Lepanto. It was not. For three days and four nights after that inconclusive clash the two fleets lay within a few miles of each other, glaring, and making repairs. Many of the French ships had been hulled, but they were stout, and heavier, on the whole, than the

British ships, which had suffered the most damage to their running gear.

The weather was dirty—long dark sullen seas and a great deal of rain.

No shot was fired in this time, nor was there any notable maneuvering. For men who held the fate of the Western world in their hands, these two admirals were singularly inactive. Nevertheless, the French remained between the British and the entrance to Chesapeake Bay.

On September 9, early in the morning, there hove into sight nine more French ships under Admiral de Barras, out of Newport, Rhode Island, and carrying the enormous siege guns needed for the pounding to pieces of Cornwallis's fortifications before Yorktown.

This was too much for the British, already aching from their wounds and running short of provisions, and they turned about and limped back to New York.

By this time Lord Cornwallis doubtless was wishing that he could somehow return to the Carolinas. He could not. George Washington from the Highlands of the Hudson River and the Count de Rochambeau from Newport had marched two separate armies side by side all the way to the eastern tip of Virginia, a movement that in daring, precision, and massive imagination can be compared only with Marlborough's march to the Rhine in 1708. Yorktown Peninsula was completely sealed off, while out beyond the capes the well-stocked French fleet waited, implacable.

Lord Cornwallis did the only thing he could do. He surrendered.

The Revolution was over.

Notes

1. The name was first Charles Town, after Charles II. It became Charlestown in 1719, and did not become Charleston until 1783, after the Revolution. However, since "Charleston" is so much the more familiar, it will be used throughout this book.

2. Sutherland, *Population Distribution in Colonial America*.

3. "Nowhere else in the American colonies were the different opinions so often, so continuously, and so ferociously expressed in action." Ward, *The War of the Revolution*, II, 660.

4. "Like many Americans after them, the Regulators unlawfully took up arms to establish lawful authority." Brown, *The South Carolina Regulators*, 1.

5. "That grudges remaining from the sectional conflict drove the bulk of the former Regulators into Toryism must remain doubtful. Tories and neutrals also appeared conspicuously among Charleston merchants and rice-indigo planters. In the end it was the Upcountry that offered determined, desperate resistance to British arms." Alden, *The South in the Revolution*, 152.

6. *Works*, X, 87.

7. It is perhaps worthy of remark that one of the standard histories of the Revolution, Henry Belcher's (see Bibliography), is entitled *The First American Civil War*.

8. "Perhaps no more than half the Tarheel population was firmly patriot" (Alden, *The South in the Revolution*,

pp. 196–97). It has been estimated that at one time or another about 50,000 Loyalists served in the British ranks, whether as militia or as regulars, and that about half of these were from New York. North Carolina probably would have done as well if it had been afforded a rallying place, the sort of toehold that the British had in New York City.

9. "The difficulties the leaders faced at every stage of the conflict, the coercion and violence by which thousands were forced into acquiescence or exile, and the constant dissensions which disrupted the leadership itself are sure evidence that the Revolution was at best but the work of an aggressive minority." Davidson, *Propaganda and the American Revolution*, xvi.

10. Van Tyne, *The Loyalists in the American Revolution*, 25–26.

11. A great deal of doubt has been cast upon this Mecklenburg Declaration, and there are those who question that it ever existed. No copy has survived, nor is there real proof of its adoption.

12. It might be well to remark, in anticipation, that it was to be a North Carolina man, Thomas Burke, who would move the incorporation into the Articles of Confederation of this important clause, which was to become of the very essence of the later Constitution: "Each state retains its sovereignty, freedom, and independence, and every power, jurisdiction and right, which is not by this confederation expressly delegated to the United States in Congress assembled." This was seconded by the South Carolina delegation; and the Virginia delegation was the only one to vote against it.

13. French, *The First Year of the American Revolution*, 458–59.

14. It is ironic that many of these Highlanders (though not Allan Macdonald) had been granted land in Cumberland, a county that had been named after William, Duke of

Cumberland, uncle of George III, and the man who had smashed the clans with monumental cruelty. No Scot, even though he had fought on the Hanoverian side, could help but hate the Butcher of Culloden. There was also named after this unattractive person, at about this time, a flower, the Sweet William; but Scots persisted in calling it the Stinking Billie.

15. Roughly, the present Fayetteville.

16. He was no relation to General William Howe or Admiral Lord Richard Howe, brothers, of England. He was to become a major general in the Continental Army.

17. Meyer, *The Highland Scots of North Carolina*, 44.

18. "Large shot, but smaller than buckshot, used for hunting large fowl, small game, and occasionally used in battle." Boatner, *Encyclopedia of the American Revolution*, 1085.

19. The most complete account of this action, and a good one, is Professor Rankin's in the *North Carolina Historical Review* (January, 1953) XXX, 23-60.

20. Moultrie, *Memoirs* . . . , I, 141.

21. Ibid., I, 143.

22. Naval theorists of the time, enamored of the huge cannons and the stability of their floating platforms, drunk with their belief in firepower, always were free with predictions of the might of their bombardments. *Nothing* could resist the full turning on of their artillery, they said again and again; and when something did—as in the case of Charleston—when men rose out of the ruins, men who were ready to go on fighting, though they should have been dead, the experts were flabbergasted. An analogy with the cocksureness of the Air Force men of today suggests itself.

23. Ward, *The War of the Revolution*, II, 677.

24. They were not to become a single entity until by a treaty with Spain in 1821 they were both taken in by the United States as a territory. At the time of the Revolution

they were invariably called "the Floridas." At that time too, and though East Jersey and West Jersey had been joined under one colonial government for almost one hundred years, New Jersey still was being referred to as "the Jerseys."

25. The Savannah Parochial Committee, in the eyes of all Loyalists an illegal body, was in actual charge of almost everything in the colony at this time. Its chairman, a highly efficient one, was Mordecai Sheftall, who must have been one of the very few Jews south of the Mason-Dixon Line. Coleman, *The American Revolution in Georgia*, 63.

26. It must be assumed that his business affairs were in poor order and that he spent most of the night preceding the duel burning his papers, so little did he leave. Only one complete letter, written and signed by him, survives. There are only thirty-six copies of his signature, and twenty-four of these, being in the possession of institutions, are not likely ever to go on the autograph market. The last one to be sold, at a public auction, fetched $14,000 (*New York Times*, June 2, 1957), and it has been asserted that if one were to appear today it could go for as much as $50,000. The reason is, of course, that so many autograph collectors seek to have a complete file of the Declaration of Independence signers. The only other signer the value of whose autograph is in any way comparable to that of Gwinnett is another man who was comparatively obscure in his time, Thomas Lynch, Jr., of South Carolina. Jenkins, *Button Gwinnett*, Chapter XIX.

27. The poet's grandfather.

28. One of these, one of the lowliest, was Henri Christophe, who was to become King of Haiti.

29. Moore, *Songs and Ballads of the American Revolution*, 273.

30. Knyphausen had his headquarters in what was then called the Robert Morris House, a mansion in Harlem that had served as a headquarters for Washington before the Continental troops had been driven out of New York. Today

it is called the Jumel Mansion, and it is a museum, located on West 160th Street between St. Nicholas and Edgecombe avenues.

31. Huger and his four equally famous brothers, Patriots all, Francis, Benjamin, Daniel, and John, were of Huguenot extraction, and they always insisted that their name be pronounced *Oo*-gee.

32. The killed-and-wounded figures were comparatively small, since there had been almost no open fighting—89 and 138 for the Americans, 76 and 189 for the British—but the loss of manpower was truly crippling. It was the biggest single American surrender until 10,700 Union troops gave themselves up to Stonewall Jackson at Harpers Ferry in 1862. Boatner, *Encyclopedia of the American Revolution*, 213.

33. "The mistake though gallant was fatal." Fortescue, III, 317.

34. He was married to the former Rebecca Calhoun, an aunt of John C. Calhoun.

35. Certainly the name was to be popularized by Mason Locke ("Parson") Weems, the inventor of the story involving Washington and the cherry tree, who wrote a "biography" of Francis Marion. Weems, never chafed by an obligation to stick to the truth, made a sort of Robin Hood out of Marion. He was not that, nor was he a Chevalier Bayard. He was a moody man, who trusted to his own intuition, which was usually sound.

36. There was nothing unusual about this. On the continent of Europe it was assumed that only aristocrats were suited to lead soldiers. The young Kalb, being ambitious, naturally inserted a "de" into his name, just as Wilhelm Steuben inserted a "von" into his. Incidentally, and for the same reason, each called himself a baron, though neither was.

37. "The plan which Gates adopted was worthy of a Caesar or a Napoleon. He did not have the talents necessary

to execute it, nor was he blessed by fortune." Alden, *The South in the Revolution*, 244.

38. This country today is considered especially salubrious, and it contains various health resorts like Pinehurst and Southern Pines. Even in de Kalb's time it was acknowledged that the air there was fine; but a man can't eat air.

39. Francis Rawdon-Hastings was not a nobleman, though he was the son of one, an Irish earl. That "lord" was a courtesy title. A product of Harrow and Oxford, he had joined the army early, and already, at twenty-six, had seen a great deal of the action in America—Bunker Hill, Monmouth, White Plains, Long Island—always with éclat, for he loved a good fight. Though he was tall and dark, he was anything but handsome; indeed, he had been called "the ugliest man in England." He could not stand General Clinton, but he got along admirably with Lord Cornwallis (who *was* a real lord), a soldier after his own heart.

40. The present Clermont, North Carolina.

41. The "in America" system of commissions—if it could be called a system—was common at this time. It somewhat corresponded to the later system of "brevet" commissions. That is, a man in the field was given, temporarily, a higher rank than the one he held at home. He did not get the higher rank's pay, and he did not displace in seniority any officers who stayed at home. This latter, of course, was the real purpose of the system, which was not a reward, only a convenience. Curtis, *The British Army in the American Revolution*.

42. The word means, literally, "huntsmen." The French word *chasseurs* means the same thing. The corps had been developed by Frederick the Great, who was always looking for new ways to kill people. It seldom acted *as* a corps, but rather in small bodies for reconnaissance, for headquarters guard duty, for advance parties, for sniping. The Jägers were generally called greencoats. They carried a rifle notably

shorter and heavier than the so-called Kentucky rifle of the American frontiersman—a weapon actually invented and developed by German immigrants in western Pennsylvania. The Jäger rifle was as accurate as the Kentucky rifle, but it would not carry quite as far. However, there were no Jägers on the Charleston expedition of 1780 anyway. About two hundred of them had been told off for this duty, under a Captain George Hanger, but they had all been aboard the *Anna,* blown across the Atlantic to be wrecked in Cornwall. Lowell, *The Hessians and Other German Auxiliaries.* . . .

43. He was the father of eighteen children, some of whom were legitimate. He was to become the first governor of Tennessee, which was then called Franklin. At the time of the Revolution, this was all a part of North Carolina.

44. Near the present-day Elizabethton, Tennessee.

45. The present Morganton, North Carolina.

46. "Ferguson's errors were political, strategic, and tactical, which is about as wrong as a soldier can get: he overestimated the Tory support and underestimated the patriot resistance in his area of responsibility; he failed to retreat when faced with defeat in detail; he failed to outpost King's Mountain, failed to fortify it for frontier-style fighting, and failed to see that his position was 'more assailable by the rifle than defensible with the bayonet,' as Henry Lee expressed it (*Memoirs,* 200)." Boatner, *Encyclopedia of the American Revolution,* 582.

47. It has sometimes been said that this was the origin of what was to become so famous, in the War Between the States, as the Rebel Yell (Fisher, *The Struggle for American Independence,* 354). This could be true. There is no evidence, however, that anybody shouted "The sword of the Lord and of Gideon."

48. A man named Robert Young was to boast for years afterward that he, with his rifle "Sweet Lips," had killed Ferguson. But eight slugs were taken out of the body, and

there might have been more. Many frontiersmen had names for their rifles, often affectionate feminine names. Daniel Boone, for example, called his, "Betsy."

49. The standard history of this battle is Lyman Draper's *King's Mountain and Its Heroes* (see Bibliography), but this is long, hard to get, and very dull. There are excellent accounts in Fisher, *The Struggle for American Independence* (II, 349–66), and Ward, *The War of the Revolution* (II, 737–47). Warmly recommended is the booklet *Kings Mountain*, by George C. Mackenzie, National Park Service Historical Handbook series No. 22.

50. Gates was to spend two years in civilian life, repeatedly petitioning Congress for a court-martial, repeatedly being turned down. At last he was tried, and cleared of all stigma of misconduct. He rejoined the army in the last years of the war, when the fighting was all over, but he was no longer an important figure.

51. Lee was twenty-six at this time, and inordinately vain. He was to marry late in life and to become the father of one of the greatest soldiers of them all—Robert E. Lee.

52. "Tarleton took a hell of a beating at Cowpens and there is nobody the Americans would rather have seen it happen to, but one more thought should be considered. What if Cornwallis had been at Kings Mountain where Tarleton's plan called for him to be? Is it not possible that Tarleton's defeat would have resulted in giving Cornwallis time to destroy Morgan as he retreated? Is it not likely that Greene could then have been defeated in detail?" Boatner, *Encyclopedia of the American Revolution*, 299.

53. "Cornwallis and his officers never changed their tactics to meet the Morgan methods, except to become more desperate in their bayonet charges. They were neither tacticians nor strategists. They had none of General Howe's skill at flanking movements by which he twice defeated Washington. They appear to have known nothing but a direct

frontal attack, and they usually made it with such a narrow column that its flanks could be enveloped." Fisher, *The Struggle for American Independence*, II, 387.

54. "In truth, the victory, though a brilliant feat of arms, was no victory. . . . Cornwallis had gained no solid advantage to compensate for the sacrifice of life, and he was now too weak farther to prosecute his mad design." Fortescue, *History of the British Army*, III, 380.

55. It had been renamed only a few years earlier after the Lord Camden who had spoken out so firmly in Parliament for the cause of the American colonies. Previously it had been called Pine Tree Hill.

Glossary of Eighteenth-Century Military Terms

ABATIS. A roadblock that was made of chopped-down trees piled on top of one another, the branches toward the oncoming or expected enemy.

BARBETTE. A wooden or earthen platform inside a fortification, on which the cannons were placed in order to allow them to shoot over the rampart.

BASTION. A projecting masonry work, usually V-shaped, on the wall of a fort, outside. From it, attackers along the CURTAIN could be cross-fired.

BLUNDERBUSS. A short chunky weapon, a musket, featured by a huge bell-shaped muzzle. The blunderbuss could discharge a lethal shower of stones, nails, lead slugs, what-have-you—but only for a short distance. Despite the popular picture, it seems certain that none of the Pilgrim Fathers carried blunderbusses. Why should they? The blunderbuss was no good as a bird gun, and any reasonably nimble Indian could hurl his tomahawk ten times the distance that a blunderbuss would carry. The blunderbuss was good only at close quarters, where its enormous muzzle had a frightening effect. It was favored by the drivers of stagecoaches and by householders who had some cause to expect burglars. It was never, properly, a military weapon, though it might sometimes be used, *ad terrorum*, in hit-and-run raids.

BROWN BESS was the nickname of a musket introduced into the British Army in 1682 and which, with minor modifications, continued to be the official arm until 1842. It was, for the time, unexpectedly short and light; and it was efficient. That it was not accurate did not trouble war-makers, who placed all emphasis upon controlled mass fire rather than upon marksmanship. It could be reloaded very quickly. The gun had a naturally brown walnut stock, while its barrels and other metal parts had been artificially browned with acid: hence the name.

CANISTER was a canvas or cloth bag filled with small round lead or iron pellets and crammed into a cannon on top of a charge of gunpowder. It would not carry as far as solid shot, but it was deadly at close quarters.

CARCASS. Nothing to do with a cadaver. It was a metal can punched with holes and filled with oiled rags that were set ablaze when the carcass was shot from a cannon. The purpose, of course, was to cause a building or a whole town to catch fire. During the Revolution, carcasses were used from warships in the Battle of Bunker Hill to destroy the deserted village of Charlestown, which in the beginning had harbored snipers. It was not very effective in that particular brush, and Marines had to be landed with old-fashioned torches to finish the job.

CASE SHOT. Another name for CANISTER.

CHEVAUX-DE-FRISE. A crisscross of heavy timbers, usually tipped with steel spikes, calculated to stop infantry. Sometimes, however, this was used underwater in an effort to prevent ships from passing a certain point.

COHORN was one of the few words in the military vocabulary of the time that was not French. It, and the weapon—a small stubby howitzer—were originally Dutch: *coehoorn.*

COUNTERSCARP. The outer wall or slope of the ditch surrounding a fort. The inner wall was the SCARP.

CURTAIN. The wall of a fortification between BASTION, towers, or other crossfire projections.

DEMILUNES were half-moon-shaped outworks, not large.

EMBRASURE. An opening in a PARAPET through which a cannon is fired.

EPAULEMENT. The "shoulder" of a fort wall; the place where the CURTAIN and BASTION meet.

FASCINES were bundles of twigs and sticks hastily assembled and tied together. They were used for constructing gun platforms and, even more, for filling ditches to permit the passage of

Glossary of Eighteenth-Century Military Terms 161

military vehicles. From such a bundle, the symbol of ancient Rome, came the name of the late unlamented fascists.

FEU DE JOIE. This was a musket salute performed by two double files, every other man firing the first time, the rest the second time on the way back. It was a complicated business.

FLANK COMPANIES. In each British infantry regiment there were a company of grenadiers (who no longer carried grenades) and a company of so-called light infantry, and these were traditionally placed upon the flanks. They were elite troops. When there was an especially dangerous or delicate mission to perform, the flank companies were pulled out of various regiments.

FLÈCHE. A small defensive ditch, unroofed, in the shape of an arrowhead, the point toward the expected enemy. (The word means "arrow" in French.) It was an outwork, a deterrent, a stopgap, not a real fortlet.

GABIONS were baskets made of any material, wicker being preferred, and filled with earth and stones. Clumsy, heavy things, they were used for shoring up parapets, filling ditches, protecting field guns. They were the eighteenth-century equivalent of sandbags.

GRAPE or GRAPESHOT was similar to CANISTER except that the balls were smaller and there were more of them.

HOWITZER meant then exactly what it does today: a smallish cannon sharply uptilted, used, mostly in mountain warfare, to lob shells or balls into a protected position.

MAHAM TOWER. A square, log fighting tower with a parapeted top slightly higher than the walls of the fort under siege. It was devised, presumably, by Colonel Hezekiah Maham.

MANTELET. A portable breastwork used to protect big guns being drawn up during a siege.

MATROSS. A sort of assistant artilleryman who helped to handle a fieldpiece in action. He was a regular member of the army, not like the horse drivers who, in both armies, were hired civilians and who retired when the guns began to boom—if not sooner.

MORTAR. Just what it is now—a short large-calibered piece of ordnance so trunnioned that it can shoot very high.

PARAPET. The wall of a fortification.
PICKET. A small party of foot soldiers sent forth in advance of the army to feel out the enemy and harass him if he approaches.
POUNDAGE. Field guns, whether on ship or ashore, were rated by the weight of the balls they could fire, which were reckoned in pounds avoirdupois. Thus, four-pounder, six-pounder, etc. This applied only to solid ball, not to CANISTER or GRAPE or CARCASSES.
RAMPART. Parapet.
RAVELIN. This was a small earthwork, an outwork, with only two faces, something like a FLÈCHE.
REDAN. It would take an expert to distinguish this from a RAVELIN, though it might be somewhat smaller.
REDOUBT. This was larger and stronger. It might be a square or some other multiangled shape, but it was always completely enclosed, never open at one end.
SAUCISSON. This, in French, means a large or German-type sausage. In eighteenth-century armies it meant a large FASCINE of roughly that shape.
SPONTOON. This was a sort of halberd or pike carried by sergeants on both sides, for protection purposes, when battle was expected. Often too these were carried by officers, whose toothpicky swords could scarcely be expected to prevail against an infantryman with a six-foot musket *and* bayonet.
TENAILLE. A small, low fortification, sometimes with only one entrance, sometimes with two, occasionally roofed, placed for annoyance purposes outside the CURTAIN between two BASTIONS.
UP IN THE AIR. An unprotected flank was said to have been left "up in the air."

Bibliography

ADAIR, DOUGLASS, see OLIVER, PETER.
ALDEN, JOHN RICHARD. *John Stuart and the Southern Colonial Frontier.* Ann Arbor: The University of Michigan Press, 1944.
——. *The American Revolution, 1775–1783.* New York: Harper and Brothers, 1954.
——. *The First South.* Baton Rouge: Louisiana State University Press, 1957.
——. *The South in the Revolution, 1763–1789.* Baton Rouge: Louisiana State University Press, 1957.
ALDEN, JOHN RICHARD, see WARD, CHRISTOPHER.
ALLEN, GARDNER W. *A Naval History of the American Revolution.* 2 vols. Boston: Houghton Mifflin Company, 1913.
ANDERSON, TROYER STEELE. *The Command of the Howe Brothers During the American Revolution.* New York and London: The Oxford University Press, 1936.
BALCH, THOMAS. *The French in America During the War of Independence of the United States, 1777–1883.* 2 vols. A translation by Thomas Willing Balch of *Les Français en Amérique Pendant la Guerre de l'Indépendance des Estats-Unis.* Philadelphia: Porter and Coates, 1891.
BANCROFT, GEORGE. *History of the United States of America.* 6 vols. New York: D. Appleton and Company, 1883.
BASS, ROBERT D. *The Green Dragon: The Lives of Banastre Tarleton and Mary Robinson.* New York: Henry Holt and Company, 1957.
BASSETT, JOHN S. "The Regulators of North Carolina." American Historical Association *Annual Report,* 1894. Washington: 1895.
BAUERMEISTER, see UHLENDORF, BERNHARD.
BELCHER, HENRY. *The First American Civil War.* 2 vols. London: The Macmillan Company, 1911.

BOATNER, MARK MAYO, III. *Encyclopedia of the American Revolution.* New York: David McKay Company, Inc., 1966.

BOTTA, CHARLES. *History of the War of Independence of the United States.* 2 vols. New Haven: Whiting, 1837.

BRIDENBAUGH, CARL. *Myths and Realities: Societies of the Colonial South.* Baton Rouge: Louisiana State University Press, 1952.

BROWN, MARVIN L., JR., see RIEDESEL, FRIEDERKE.

BROWN, RICHARD MAXWELL. *The South Carolina Regulators: The Story of the First American Vigilante Movement.* Cambridge: Harvard University Press, 1963.

BROWN, WALLACE. *The King's Friends: The Composition and Motives of the American Loyalist Claimants.* Providence: Brown University Press, 1965.

CALLAHAN, NORTH. *Daniel Morgan: Ranger of the Revolution.* New York: Holt, Rinehart and Winston, 1961.

——. *Flight from the Republic: The Tories of the American Revolution.* Indianapolis: The Bobbs-Merrill Company, Inc., 1967.

CARRINGTON, HENRY B. *Battles of the American Revolution, 1775–1781.* New York: A. S. Barnes and Company, 1876.

CHANNING, EDWARD. *A History of the United States.* 6 vols. New York: The Macmillan Company, 1905–1925.

CLINTON, SIR HENRY. *The American Rebellion: Sir Henry Clinton's Narrative of His Campaigns, 1775–1782.* Edited by William B. Willcox. New Haven: Yale University Press, 1961.

COLEMAN, KENNETH. *The American Revolution in Georgia, 1763–1789.* Athens: University of Georgia Press, 1958.

CORWIN, EDWARD S. *French Policy and the American Alliance of 1778.* Princeton: Princeton University Press, 1916.

CURTIS, E. E. *The British Army in the American Revolution.* New Haven: Yale University Press, 1926.

DAVIDSON, PHILIP. *Propaganda and the American Revolution, 1763–1783.* Chapel Hill: The University of North Carolina Press, 1941.

DAWSON, HENRY BARTON. *Battles of the United States by Sea and Land.* 2 vols. New York: Johnson, Fry and Company, 1858.

DE MOND, ROBERT O. *The Loyalists in North Carolina During the Revolution.* Durham: Duke University Press, 1940.

Bibliography 165

DOUGLASS, ELISHA P. *Rebels and Democrats: The Struggle for Equal Political Rights and Majority Rule During the American Revolution.* Chapel Hill: University of North Carolina Press, 1955.

DOYLE, JOSEPH B. *Frederick William von Steuben and the American Revolution.* Steubenville, Ohio: The H. C. Cook Co., 1913.

DRAPER, LYMAN C. *King's Mountain and Its Heroes.* Cincinnati: Peter G. Thomson, 1881.

EARLE, EDWARD MEADE. *Makers of Modern Strategy.* Princeton: Princeton University Press, 1943.

ECKENRODE, HAMILTON JAMES. *The Revolution in Virginia.* Boston: Houghton Mifflin Company, 1916.

EINSTEIN, CAVIS. *Divided Loyalties: Americans in England During the War of Independence.* London: Cobden-Sanderson, 1933.

EMMONS, G. F. *The Navy of the United States, 1775–1853.* Washington: Gideon & Company, 1853.

ESPOSITO, COL. VINCENT J., editor. *The West Point Atlas of American Wars.* New York: Frederick A. Praeger, 1959.

FINLEY, JOHN H. *The Coming of the Scot.* New York: Charles Scribner's Sons, 1940.

FISHER, SYDNEY GEORGE. *The Struggle for American Independence.* 2 vols. Philadelphia: J. B. Lippincott Company, 1908.

FISKE, JOHN. *The American Revolution.* 2 vols. Boston: Houghton Mifflin Company, 1891.

FITZPATRICK, JOHN CLEMENT, see WASHINGTON, GEORGE.

FORTESCUE, JOHN W. *History of the British Army.* 10 vols. New York: The Macmillan Company, 1899–1920.

FREEMAN, DOUGLAS SOUTHALL. *George Washington: A Biography.* 6 vols. New York: Charles Scribner's Sons, 1948–1954.

FRENCH, ALLEN. *The First Year of the American Revolution.* Boston: Houghton Mifflin Company, 1934.

FULLER, J. F. C. *Decisive Battles of the U.S.A.* New York: Thomas Yoseloff, 1942.

GAMBLE, THOMAS. *Savannah Duels and Duellists, 1733–1877.* Savannah: Review Publishing Company, 1923.

GANOE, WILLIAM ADDLEMAN. *The History of the United States*

Army. New York and London: D. Appleton-Century Company, 1943.

GOTTSCHALK, LOUIS. *Lafayette and the Close of the American Revolution.* Chicago: University of Chicago Press, 1942.

GRAHAM, JAMES. *The Life of General Daniel Morgan, of the Virginia Line of the Army of the United States.* New York: Derby and Jackson, 1856.

GRANGER, BRUCE INGHAM. *Political Satire in the American Revolution, 1763–1783.* Ithaca, N.Y.: Cornell University Press, 1960.

GREENE, FRANCIS VINTON. *General Greene.* New York: D. Appleton and Company, 1893.

———. *The Revolutionary War and the Military Policy of the United States.* New York: Charles Scribner's Sons, 1911.

GREENE, GEORGE WASHINGTON. *The Life of Nathanael Greene, Major-General in the Army of the Revolution.* 3 vols. New York: G. P. Putnam and Son, 1867 (Vol. I); Hurd and Houghton, 1871 (Vols. II and III).

HATCH, LOUIS CLINTON. *The Administration of the American Revolutionary Army.* New York: Longmans, Green and Company, 1904.

HENDERSON, ARCHIBALD. "The Origin of the Regulation in North Carolina." *American Historical Review,* XXI, 1915–1916.

HENDRICK, BURTON J. *The Lees of Virginia: Biography of a Family.* Boston: Little, Brown and Company, 1941.

HIGGINBOTHAM, DON. *Daniel Morgan, Revolutionary Rifleman.* Chapel Hill: University of North Carolina Press, 1961.

HOOKER, RICHARD J., see WOODMASON, CHARLES.

HUDSON, ARTHUR P. "Songs of the North Carolina Regulators." *William and Mary Quarterly,* 3rd series, IV, 1947.

HUTH, MARTA, see RIEDESEL, FRIEDERKE.

JAMES, WILLIAM DOBEIN. *A Sketch of the Life of Brigadier General Francis Marion.* Marietta, Ga.: Continental Book Company, 1948.

JAMESON, J. FRANKLIN. *The American Revolution Considered as a Social Movement.* Princeton: Princeton University Press, 1926.

JENKINS, CHARLES FRANCIS. *Button Gwinnett, Signer of the Decla-*

ration of Independence. Garden City: Doubleday, Page & Company, 1926.

JOHNSON, HENRY P. *The Yorktown Campaign and the Surrender of Cornwallis.* New York: Harper and Brothers, 1881.

JOHNSON, WILLIAM. *Sketches of the Life and Correspondence of Nathanael Greene, Major General of the Armies of the United States in the War of the Revolution.* 2 vols. Charleston: Published by the author, 1822.

KAPP, FRIEDRICH. *The Life of John Kalb, Major-General in the Revolutionary War.* New York: Henry Holt and Company, 1884.

———. *The Life of Frederick William von Steuben, Major General in the Revolutionary Army.* New York: Mason Brothers, 1859.

KAUFFMAN, HENRY J. *The Pennsylvania-Kentucky Rifle.* New York: Bonanza Books, 1960.

KNOLLENBERG, BERNHARD. *Washington and the Revolution: A Reappraisal.* New York: The Macmillan Company, 1940.

LANDERS, H. L. *The Battle of Camden, South Carolina.* Washington: Government Printing Office, 1929.

LARRABEE, HAROLD A. *Decision at the Chesapeake.* New York: Clarkson N. Potter, Inc., 1964.

LEE, HENRY. *Campaign of 1781 in the Carolinas.* Philadelphia: Littell, William Brown, 1824.

LEFFERTS, CHARLES W. *Uniforms of the American, British, French, and German Armies in the War of the American Revolution, 1775–1783.* Edited by Alexander J. Wall. New York: The New-York Historical Society, 1926.

LEFLER, HUGH TALMADGE, and ALBERT RAY NEWSOME. *North Carolina: The History of a Southern State.* Chapel Hill: The University of North Carolina Press, 1954.

LOSSING, B. L. *Pictorial Field Book of the Revolution.* 2 vols. New York: Harper & Brothers, 1859.

LOWELL, EDWARD J. *The Hessians and Other German Auxiliaries of Great Britain in the Revolutionary War.* New York: Harper & Brothers, 1884.

McConkey, Rebecca. *The Hero of Cowpens: A Revolutionary Sketch.* New York and London: Funk & Wagnalls, 1885.

MacKenzie, George C. *Kings Mountain National Military Park.* Washington: National Park Service, 1961.

Mahan, Alfred Thayer. *The Influence of Sea Power upon History, 1660–1783.* Boston: Little, Brown and Company, 1894.

———. *The Major Operations of the Navies in the War of American Independence.* New York: Burt Franklin, 1913.

Meyer, Duane. *The Highland Scots of North Carolina, 1732–1776.* Chapel Hill: University of North Carolina Press, 1957.

Montross, Lynn. *Rag, Tag, and Bobtail: The Story of the Continental Army.* New York: Harper and Brothers, 1952.

Moore, Frank. *Songs and Ballads of the American Revolution.* New York: D. Appleton and Company, 1856.

Moultrie, William. *Memoirs of the American Revolution, So Far as It Related to the States of North and South Carolina, and Georgia.* 2 vols. New York: D. Longworth, 1802.

Mowat, Charles Loch. *East Florida as a British Province, 1763–1784.* Gainesville: The University of Florida Press, 1964.

Nelson, William H. *The American Tory.* Oxford: The Clarendon Press, 1961.

Nevins, Allan. *The American States During and After the Revolution, 1775–1798.* New York: The Macmillan Company, 1927.

Newsome, Albert Ray, see Lefler, Hugh Talmadge.

Oliver, Peter. *Origin and Progress of the American Revolution: A Tory View.* Edited by Douglass Adair and John A. Schutz. San Marino, Calif.: The Huntington Library, 1961.

Oswald, Richard. *Memorandum on the Folly of Invading Virginia, etc.* Charlottesville: University Press of Virginia, 1953.

Palmer, John McAuley. *General von Steuben.* New Haven: Yale University Press, 1937.

Peckham, Howard H. *The War of Independence: A Military History.* Chicago: University of Chicago Press, 1958.

Rankin, Hugh F. "The Moore's Creek Bridge Campaign, 1776." *North Carolina Historical Review,* XXX, January 1953.

Richeson, Charles R. *British Politics and the American Revolution.* Norman: University of Oklahoma Press, 1954.

Riedesel, Friederke C. von. *Baroness von Riedesel and the*

American Revolution: Journal and Correspondence of a Tour of Duty, 1776–1783. Translated, with an introduction and notes, by Marvin L. Brown, Jr., with the assistance of Marta Huth. Chapel Hill: University of North Carolina Press, 1965.

ROBERTS, KENNETH. *The Battle of Cowpens.* Garden City, N.Y.: Doubleday and Company, Inc., 1958.

ROBSON, ERIC. *The American Revolution in Its Political and Military Aspects, 1763–1783.* London: The Batchworth Press, 1955.

RUSSELL, CARL P. *Guns on the Early Frontiers: A History of Firearms from Colonial Times Through the Years of the Western Fur Trade.* Berkeley and Los Angeles: University of California Press, 1957.

SABINE, LORENZO. *Biographical Sketches of Loyalists of the American Revolution.* 2 vols. Boston: Little, Brown and Company, 1864.

SCHLESINGER, ARTHUR MEIER. "The American Revolution Reconsidered." *Political Science Quarterly,* XXXIV, 61–78.

———. *The Colonial Merchants and the American Revolution.* New York: The Facsimile Library, 1939.

SCHUTZ, JOHN A., *see* OLIVER, PETER.

SHY, JOHN. *Toward Lexington: The Role of the British Army in the Coming of the American Revolution.* Princeton: Princeton University Press, 1965.

SIMCOE, LIEUT. COL., J.G. *A History of the Operations of a Partisan Corps, Called The Queen's Rangers, Commanded by Lieut. Col. J. G. Simcoe, During the War of the American Revolution.* New York: The New York Times and Arno Press, Inc., 1968. (Reprint of the original edition published by Bartlett & Welford, New-York, 1844.)

SIMMS, WILLIAM G. *The Life of Nathanael Greene, Major-General in the Army of the Revolution.* Philadelphia: Leary and Getz, 1849.

STEDMAN, CHARLES. *The History of the Origin, Progress, and Termination of the American War.* 2 vols. London: Printed for the author, 1794.

STEELE, MATTHEW F. *American Campaigns.* 2 vols. Washington: Byron S. Adams, 1909.

STEVENS, BENJAMIN FRANKLIN, editor. *The Clinton-Cornwallis Controversy.* 2 vols. London, 1880.

STEVENS, WILLIAM OLIVER. *Pistols at Ten Paces: The Code of Honor in America.* Boston: Houghton Mifflin Company, 1940.

SUTHERLAND, STELLA H. *Population Distribution in Colonial America.* New York: Columbia University Press, 1956.

TARLETON, BANASTRE. *A History of the Campaigns of 1780 and 1781, in the Southern Provinces of North America.* London: T. Cadell, 1787.

THAYER, THEODORE. *Nathanael Greene, Strategist of the American Revolution.* New York: Twayne Publishers, 1960.

TOWER, CHARLEMAGNE. *The Marquis de la Fayette in the American Revolution.* 2 vols. Philadelphia: J. B. Lippincott Company, 1901.

TREACY, M. F. *Prelude to Yorktown: The Southern Campaign of Nathanael Greene, 1780–1781.* Chapel Hill: University of North Carolina Press, 1963.

TREVELYAN, GEORGE OTTO. *The American Revolution.* 6 vols. London: Longmans, Green and Company, 1905.

TYLER, MOSES COIT. "The Party of the Loyalists in the American Revolution." *American Historical Review,* October 1895.

———. *The Literary History of the American Revolution.* 2 vols. New York: G. P. Putnam's Sons, 1897.

UHLENDORF, BERNHARD A., editor. *Revolution in America: Confidential Letters and Journals, 1776–1784, of Adjutant General Major Bauermeister of the Hessian Forces.* New Brunswick, N.J.: Rutgers University Press, 1957.

VAN TYNE, CLAUDE HALSTEAD. *The American Revolution.* New York: Harper and Brothers, 1905.

———. *England and America, Rivals in the American Revolution.* Cambridge: Cambridge University Press, 1929.

———. *The Loyalists in the American Revolution.* New York: Peter Smith, 1929.

WALL, ALEXANDER J., *see* LEFFERTS, CHARLES W.

WALLACE, WILLARD M. *Appeal to Arms: A Military History of the American Revolution.* New York: Harper and Brothers, 1951.

WARD, CHRISTOPHER. *The War of the Revolution.* 2 vols. Edited by John Richard Alden. New York: The Macmillan Company, 1952.

WASHINGTON, GEORGE. *The Writings of George Washington, from the Original Manuscript Sources, 1745–1799.* Edited by John Clement Fitzpatrick. Washington: U.S. Government Printing Office, 1931–1944.

WHARTON, FRANCIS, editor. *Revolutionary Correspondence of the United States.* 6 vols. Washington: Government Printing Office, 1889.

WHITE, KATHERINE KEOGH. *The King's Mountain Men: The Story of the Battle, with Sketches of the American Soldiers Who Took Part.* Baltimore: Genealogical Publishing Company, 1966.

WHITLOCK, BRAND. *Lafayette.* 2 vols. New York: D. Appleton and Company, 1929.

WILLCOX, JAMES. "The British Road to Yorktown: A Study in Divided Command." *American Historical Review,* LII, October 1946.

WILLCOX, WILLIAM B., see CLINTON, SIR HENRY.

WOODMASON, CHARLES. *The Carolina Backcountry on the Eve of the Revolution.* Edited with an introduction by Richard J. Hooker. Chapel Hill: University of North Carolina Press, 1953.

WRIGHT, MARCUS J. "Lafayette's Campaign in Virginia, April–October, 1781." *Publications of the Southern History Association,* IX, 1905.

Index

Actaeon, H.M.S., 42, 45–46
Active, H.M.S., 42
Adams, John, 18
André, Major John, 70
Arbuthnot, Admiral Marriott, 74
Armand, Colonel Charles, 93
Arnold, Benedict, 22, 57, 101, 116, 125, 137
Ashe, Colonel John, 30, 31

Barras, Admiral de Saint-Laurent, Comte de, 149
Barron, Captain James, 39
Boone, Daniel, 125, note 48
Braddock, Major General Edward, 125, 129
Bristol, H.M.S., 42, 43
Brown, Thomas, 52
Buford, Colonel Abraham, 80, 81
Bullock, Archibald, 53
Burgoyne, Major General John, 56, 91, 138
Burke, Thomas, note 12

Camden, Battle of, 93–99
Campbell, Lieutenant Colonel Archibald, 58–61
Campbell, Lieutenant Colonel Donald, 10
Campbell, Captain John, 32
Campbell, Colonel William, 108–109, 111–112
Carleton, Sir Guy, 35
Carroll, Charles, of Carrollton, 20
Caswell, Colonel Richard, 31–32
Charleston, 15, 16, 22; siege of, 39–43; 59, 70–76, notes 1 and 22
Clark, Elijah, 61
Cleveland, Colonel Benjamin, 108
Clinton, Lieutenant General Sir Edward, 36–37, 42–43, 45, 47–48, 50, 56–58, 70–71, 74–75, 78, 80, 84, 101, note 39
Cornwallis, Major General Charles, Lord, 38, 42, 71, 80, 81, 83, 84, 94–96; takes command in South, 100–105; 108–109, 111, 119, 120, 123–127, 134, 136–139, 140–142, 144–145, 147–149, notes 39, 52, 53, 54

Cowpens, Battle of, 109, 128–129, 130–134, 136, 139, note 52
Cruzier, H.M.S., 27

Dartmouth, Earl of, 35, 36
Davidson, Brigadier General William, 108, 123
Dillon, General, 66
Doak, Reverend Samuel, 107
Dooly, John, 61
Dunmore, Governor John Murray, Lord, 27

Eden, Governor Robert, 38
Elbert, Lieutenant Colonel Samuel, 54
Estaing, Admiral-General Jean-Baptiste Charles Henri Hector Theodat, Comte d', 62–67
Experiment, H.M.S., 42–43

Ferguson, Lieutenant Colonel Patrick, 102–106, 108–109, 110–111, 127
Friendship, H.M.S., 42

Gadsden, Christopher, 74
Gage, Lieutenant General Thomas, 25
Gates, Major General Horatio, 89, 90–96, 98–99, 116–119, 138, note 50
George III, 61, note 14
Germain, Lord George, 35, 36, 38, 47–48, 71, 101
Gist, Colonel Mordecai, 98

Glover, Brigadier General John, 116
Grasse, Admiral François-Joseph-Paul, Comte de, 148
Greene, Major General Nathanael, 89, 117–119, 121–126, 128, 136–139, 140–142, 144–147
Guilford Court House, Battle of, 136–137, 142
Gwinnett, Button, 21, 52–55, note 26

Habersham, Major Joseph, 54
Hall, Lyman, 21
Hancock, John, 20
Hanger, Captain George, note 42
Hanging Rock, Battle of, 85
Hopkins, John, 52
Howe, Admiral Richard, Lord, 63, 64
Howe, Major General Robert, 27, 30, 58–59, 60, 118
Howe, Major General Sir William, 36–37, 47–48, 50, 52, 56, 70, 71, 91, note 53
Huger, Benjamin, note 31
Huger, Daniel, note 31
Huger, Francis, note 31
Huger, Isaac, 137, note 31
Huger, John, note 31

Jackson, Andrew, 85
Jasper, Sergeant William, 45–47, 67
Jefferson, Thomas, 119

Index

Kalb, Major General Johann, Baron de, 91–92, 94, 98–99, notes 36, 38
Kerr, Joseph, 110
Kettle Creek, Battle of, 9, 12, 61, 86
King's Mountain, Battle of, 110–114, 126
Knyphausen, Lieutenant General Wilhelm von, 71, note 30
Kosciuszko, Brigadier General Tadeusz Andrszej Bonawentura, 121–122

Lee, Major General Charles, 37–39, 41–42, 45–46, 52, 90–91, 118
Lee, Lieutenant Colonel Henry, 120, 146, note 51
Lee, Robert E., note 51
Leslie, Major General Alexander, 119, 123
Lillington, Colonel Alexander, 30, 31
Lincoln, Major General Benjamin, 58, 65, 67, 72, 74–75, 118
Lynch, Thomas, Jr., note 26

McArthur, Major, 132
McCall, Lieutenant Colonel James, 130, 132
MacDonald, Allan, 25, 29, 32, note 14
MacDonald, Colonel Donald, 26, 29, 30, 31
MacDonald, Flora, 25, 29, 32
McDowell, Colonel Charles M., 107–108, 123

McIntosh, George, 53
McIntosh, Brigadier General Lachlan, 52–54
McLeod, Alexander, 32, 33
McLeod, Donald, 27, 29
Maham, Colonel Hezekiah, 146–147
Marion, Brigadier General Francis, 87, 93, 136, note 35
Martin, Governor Josiah, 23, 25–29, 30
Mecklenburg Declaration, 21, note 11
Moncrieff, Major James, 73–74
Monroe, James, 121
Montgomery, Major General Richard, 22
Moore, Colonel James, 30, 31
Moore's Creek Bridge, Battle of, 28–34, 38, 62, 144
Morgan, Brigadier General Daniel, 108, 124–129, 130–131, 139, 141, 143, note 53
Moultrie, Brigadier General, 41–43, 46–47, 64, note 20
Muhlenberg, Brigadier General Peter, 116

Parker, Commodore Hyde, 59
Parker, Admiral Sir Peter, 38–39, 43–44, 47
Peyster, Captain Abraham de, 113
Philips, Samuel, 104
Phillips, Major General William, 137–138, 147
Pickens, Brigadier General Andrew, 11, 61, 85, 128, 130

Prevost, Brigadier General Augustine, 50, 53, 58, 61, 65
Provost, Lieutenant Colonel James Mark, 61
Pulaski, Count Casimir, 66, 93

Rawdon, Brigadier General Francis Rawdon-Hastings, Lord, 73, 95, 145–147, note 39
Regulators, the, 15–17, 23, 29, 33, notes 4, 5
Rochambeau, Jean-Baptiste Donatien de Vimeur, Comte de, 149
Rogers, Major Robert, 51
Rutledge, Governor John, 39, 41, 64, 74

Saunders, Hiram, 109
Scarborough, H.M.S., 51
Schuyler, Major General Philip, 38
Sevier, Colonel John, 106, 108
Sheftall, Mordecai, note 25
Shelby, Colonel Isaac, 104, 108, 112
Simcoe, Lieutenant Colonel John Graves, 120
Smallwood, Brigadier General Alexander, 98
Solebay, H.M.S., 42, 45
Sphinx, H.M.S., 42, 45, 46
Steuben, Major General Wilhelm von, 137, note 36
Stuart, Charles Edward (the Young Pretender), 24–25
Stuart, John, 51–52

Sullivan, Major General John, 64, 67, 116
Sumpter, Brigadier General Thomas, 86–87, 93, 104, 136
Syren, H.M.S., 46

Tarleton, Lieutenant Colonel Banastre, 78–79, 80–83, 87, 97, 104, 113, 120, 126–129, 131–134
Thunder, H.M.S., 42
Tryon, Governor William, 17, 23, 25, 37

Van Tyne, Claude Halstead, 21, note 10
Ville de Paris, flagship, 148

Walton, George, 21
Washington, George, 20, 37, 38, 56–57, 63, 71–72, 89, 91, 118, 149
Washington, Captain William, 120–121, 129, 132–134, 146
Waxhaws, Battle of, 80–83
Wayne, Major General Anthony, 116
Weedon, Brigadier General George, 116
Wells, George, 54
Williams, Colonel Otho Holland, 139, 140
Winston, Major Joseph, 108
Wright, Governor Sir James, 51, 54, 58

Young, Robert, note 48

www.ingramcontent.com/pod-product-compliance
Lightning Source LLC
LaVergne TN
LVHW040116080426
835507LV00039B/392